THE
Impressionists
HANDBOOK

THE
Impressionists
HANDBOOK

THE GREAT WORKS AND THE
WORLD THAT INSPIRED THEM

ROBERT KATZ AND CELESTINE DARS

HERMES
HOUSE

This edition is published by Hermes House, an imprint of Anness Publishing Ltd,
108 Great Russell Street, London WC1B 3NA; info@anness.com

www.hermeshouse.com; www.annesspublishing.com; twitter: @Anness_Books

Anness Publishing has a new picture agency outlet for images for publishing, promotions
or advertising. Please visit our website www.practicalpictures.com for more information.

Publisher: Joanna Lorenz
Senior Editor: Felicity Forster
Production Controller: Stephanie Moe

PUBLISHER'S NOTE
Although the information in this book is believed to be accurate and true at the time of
going to press, neither the authors nor the publisher can accept any legal responsibility or liabil-
ity for any errors or omissions that may have been made.

PICTURE CREDITS
Baltimore, Walters Art Gallery, p.28, 169/Bridgeman Art Library; Boston, Museum of Fine Arts, p110; Bridgeman Art Library, p1, 26–7, 35, 62–3,
64, 70, 71, 72, 73, 81, 82, 84, 87, 92, 97, 100–1, 104, 108, 109, 111, 112–3, 114, 115, 117, 118, 121, 131, 133, 136, 137, 138, 139, 142–3, 145,
146–7, 152, 153, 154–5, 157, 158–9, 162–3, 165, 168, 170, 175, 178–9, 181, 183, 185, 192–3, 195, 198–9, 202, 203, 206, 208, 209, 210, 211, 213,
214, 215, 217, 218, 219, 223, 224, 225, 226, 226–7, 228–9, 230–1, 232, 233, 234, 235, 240, 241, 248–9, 250, 251, 254; Cambridge, Mass., Fogg Art
Museum, p.161, 204; Cardiff National Museum and Gallery of Wales, p.164/Visual Arts Library/Bridgeman Art Library; Chicago Art Institute,
p.11, 17, 32, 41, 54, 55, 68, 77, 99, 110, 130, 212; Chicago Art Institute, p.188–9/Bridgeman Art Library; Cincinnati Art Museum, p.24/Visual Arts
Library/Bridgeman Art Library; Cleveland Museum of Art, p.16, 237/Visual Art Library/Bridgeman Art Library; Copenhagen Ny Carlsberg
Glyptotek, p.151; Dijon, Musée des Beaux-Arts, p.150; Genova, Palazzo Rosso, 69/Visual Arts Library; Glasgow Burrell Collection,
p.184/Bridgeman Art Library; Kansas City Nelson-Atkins Museum of Art, p.103/Bridgeman Art Library; London Christie's Images, p.47, 49, 56,
106–7, 129, 134–5, 148, 200, 238/Bridgeman Art Library; London National Gallery, p.22–3, 85, 130, 167, 187/Bridgeman Art Library; London
Noortman Ltd. p.8/Bridgeman Art Library; London Tate Gallery, p.186; London Victoria & Albert Museum, p.21/Visual Art Library/Bridgeman
Art Library; Los Angeles County Museum of Art, p.204/ Visual Arts Library/Bridgeman Art Library; Lyon, Musée des Beaux-Arts, p182; Madrid
Prado, p.75/Index/Bridgeman Art Library; Nancy, Musée des Beaux-Arts, p171; New York Metropolitan Museum of Art, p.14, 164,
204/Bridgeman Art Library; New York Metropolitan Museum of Art, p43, 50, 96/Visual Art Library/Bridgeman Art Library, 72/Edimedia;
Oberlin Museum of Art, p76; Paris, Bibliothèque Nationale, p60/Visual Arts Library; Paris Louvre, p.20, 34–5/Bridgeman Art Library, 57,
61/Edimedia, p110/Giraudon; Paris Musée d'Orsay, p.12, 197/Bullox/Bridgeman Art Library; Musée d'Orsay, p.38–9, 102, 128, 140, 144, 166,
171, 184, 188, 190, 194, 222, 246, 247, 252/Giraudon/Bridgeman Art Library; Musée d'Orsay, p.80, 150/Lauros-Giraudon/Bridgeman Art Library;
Musée d'Orsay p.10, 15, 42, 125, 167, 173/Peter Willi/Bridgeman Art Library; Musée d'Orsay, p.44, 58/Bridgeman Art Library; Musée d'Orsay,
p.59/Visual Arts Library/Bridgeman Art Library; Musée d'Orsay, p.79, 239, 242/Bridgeman Art Library; Musée Picasso
p.184/Giraudon/Bridgeman Art Library; Pau Musée des Beaux-Arts, p.91/Bridgeman Art Library; Philadelphia Museum of Art. p.33, 103, 160,
191, 236/Visual Art Library/Bridgeman Art Library; Princetown University Art Museum, p.53/Bridgeman Art Library; Private Collections, p.119,
177; Private Collections p.18, 141, 176/Christie's Images/Bridgeman Art Library; Private Collections p.30, 31, 54, 73, 76, 78, 83, 86, 88, 94, 120,
125, 196, 216, 220, 244/Bridgeman Art Library; Private Collections, p156, 180, 186/Giraudon; Private Collections, p.201/Visual Arts
Library/Bridgeman Art Library; Washington National Gallery of Art, p.89, 101, 153, 158, 166; Washington DC National Gallery of Art p.45/Visual
Arts Library/Bridgeman Art Library; Washington DC Phillips Collection, p.174/Visual Arts Library/Bridgeman Art Library; Williamstown Clark
Institute, p.13/Visual Arts Library/Bridgeman Art Library.
EVERY EFFORT HAS BEEN MADE TO CREDIT THE COPYRIGHT OWNERS OF THE PICTURE USED.

Page 1
RENOIR
The Path in the Grass
oil on canvas
c.1875.
60 × 74cm (24 × 29in)

Page 2
DEGAS
Dancers Wearing Green Skirts
oil on canvas
c.1895.
140 × 80cm (55 × 31in)

Page 3
MONET
Green Park, London
oil on canvas
1871.
40 × 73cm (16 × 29in)

Page 4
MORISOT
Lucie Léon at the Piano
oil on canvas
1892.
65 × 80cm (26 × 32in)

CONTENTS

SECTION ONE

·

A HISTORY OF
IMPRESSIONISM

FRANCE AND IMPRESSIONISM

T HE IMPRESSIONISTS DID NOT choose their name – it was foisted upon them in 1874 by a critic hostile to their work. However the name soon stuck and was used to describe a group of artists who never intended to be a unified radical movement, who never set out to shock or be revolutionaries. What they had in common was that they were all in Paris in the early 1860s and quickly got to know each other – some in art schools which they abandoned early on, some in the cafés where they would meet – and realized that they shared a desire to paint the landscape, cityscape, and modern life in new ways. The first Impressionist exhibition took place because none of these artists had achieved any regular success at the official Salon, the major venue for the Paris art market, whose juries were notoriously inconsistent and reactionary.

The first exhibition by this group did little to challenge the all-powerful Salon, but it crystallized critical opinion and pushed the so-called Impressionists into the limelight. They were pilloried by hostile critics and supported by writers such as Baudelaire and Zola who saw in their work an important advancement of art into the modern era. But the Impressionists did not seek to criticize their society; they were largely middle class and politically conservative in an age permanently on the brink of upheaval. They remained true to aesthetic ideas which, with few exceptions, kept them from depicting the grinding poverty caused by rapid industrial expansion, and the sporadic outbursts of war and violence that punctuated the history of their times.

JONGKIND
The Sainte Catherine's Market at Honfleur
(DETAIL)
oil on canvas
1865.
42 × 66cm
(17 × 26in)

APRIL 1874: SHOCK OF THE NEW

The Impressionist eye is, in short, the most advanced eye in human evolution . . .

JULES LAFORGUE, 1883

For one month from 15th April 1874 a new exhibition was to be seen at 35 boulevard des Capucines in Paris. Félix Nadar, a well-known photographer, had lent his studio free of charge to a group of artists who had come together as the *Société anonyme des artistes peintres, sculpteurs, graveurs, etc.* (a joint stock company of artists, painters, etc.). The show was open from ten to six during the day and eight to ten at night for an admission price of one franc. Among the twenty-nine artists showing their work were Paul Cézanne, Edgar Degas, Armand Guillaumin, Claude Monet, Berthe Morisot, Camille Pissarro, Pierre-Auguste Renoir, and Alfred Sisley.

The show was rapidly becoming a disaster. The members of the *Société anonyme* who had banded together to stage the show had of course aimed to generate sales as well as a greater awareness of their work with the public. Around 3,500 people visited the exhibition before it closed on 15th May but very few pictures were bought – the work of Degas and Morisot remained unsold, whilst Renoir had to knock down the price of his painting *La Loge* from 500 to 425 francs before he could sell it. In general the public came for the novelty value, to see a cause *célèbre* in the making. Only the critics were triumphant. Writing in the satirical journal *Charivari* on 25th April 1874, Louis Leroy, a minor critic and playwright, composed an acerbic satirical review of the exhibition in the form of a tour around it in the company of an imaginary landscape

painter called Joseph Vincent. Having relentlessly debunked most of the other artists on show, Leroy devoted part of the climax of his satire to a picture by Claude Monet:

A catastrophe seemed to be imminent, and it was reserved for M. Monet to contribute the last straw.

"Ah, there he is!" he cried, in front of No.98. "I recognize him, papa Vincent's favourite! What does that canvas depict? Look at the catalogue."

"*Impression, Sunrise.*"

"*Impression* – I was sure of it. I was just telling myself that, since I was impressed, there had to be some impression in it . . . and what freedom, what ease of workmanship! Wallpaper in its embryonic state is more finished than this seascape."

Monet had chosen the title of this picture in some haste for the exhibition catalogue, not wanting to call it a simple "seascape", and in doing so he had unwittingly provided Leroy with the hook-line for his piece. The review appeared under the headline *Exhibition of the Impressionists*. Leroy had coined a name which would be certain to outlive his own.

What were these so-called Impressionists doing that was so unacceptable? Leroy had put his finger on the obvious qualities of one

CAMILLE PISSARRO
Self-portrait
1873.

aspect of their work, what henceforth would be called the "Impressionist" use of paint – a method that was as shocking as it was new to its public. Standing in front of Monet's *Boulevard des Capucines,* Leroy's imaginary companion declares:

"Is that brilliant enough for you now? There's an *impression*, or I don't know what it means. Only be so good as to tell me what those innumerable black tongue-lickings in the lower part of the picture represent?"

"Why, those are people walking along," I replied.

Leroy, of course, could read the painting and see the effect that Monet's brushwork intended to convey, but a tradition of officially-sanctioned, respected and respectable Salon painting – which stressed the suitability of subject, quality and finesse of finish – inevitably meant that the public were looking at Monet's *Boulevard des Capucines* and *Impression, Sunrise*, or Degas' ballerinas, with a conservative, unprepared eye. To many, all that really could be seen from a couple of feet were blotches, strokes and scrapes of compacted pigment, which viewed from a "safe" distance would then coalesce into meaningful shapes. The "Impressionist technique" (in reality each artist was developing his own), allied with a new approach to colour and a new range of subject matter, made the *Société anonyme's* first exhibition the laughing-stock of Paris. Yet it represented to the world at large a revolution in art that had been gathering since the early 1860s, when Edouard Manet caused a scandal with his *Luncheon on the Grass* (*Déjeuner sur l'herbe*).

In the early 1860s Frédéric Bazille, Monet, Renoir, and Sisley had met in Paris to study at the atelier of the Swiss painter Charles Gleyre, whilst Pissarro had come to know Monet and Paul Cézanne. The high period of Impressionism was brief; merely a decade later a somewhat diluted form of Impressionism had already been adopted by numerous conventional artists. Its influence, however, has lasted to this day.

The idea of an independent show outside the auspices of the Salon – the annual exhibition of the Académie des Beaux-Arts held in the Louvre's Salon d'Apollon and later in the enormous Palais d'Industrie – was increasingly discussed. Hitherto, the Académie des Beaux-Arts determined almost exclusively the showing of art. Without the sanction of the Salon an artist's work was practically unseen by the bourgeoisie which constituted his (and increasingly her) public. Furthermore, the atelier system of apprenticeship to a teacher who would prepare his students for the Ecole des Beaux-Arts, the teaching arm of the Académie, followed by the winning of one of the school's competitions, was the only way an artist could expect to learn and then progress in a career which depended on the patronage of conservative institutions and patrons. For good or ill, Leroy's insistence on the word "impression" tied together for posterity a group of artists whose aims were frequently at loggerheads, yet who had set out together, rejecting the Salon which had so often rejected them.

What the unimaginative public and critics like Leroy found gross and unpolished, slapdash and meaningless in the work of the Impressionists shown at Nadar's studio was exactly what later generations came to value most in it. Writing in 1883 to introduce a small

FANTIN-LATOUR
Edouard Manet
1867.

RENOIR
Claude Monet
1875.

show by Pissarro, Degas, and Renoir in Berlin, the poet Jules Laforgue (who died three years later at the age of twenty-seven) considered the Impressionists' work in a remarkable essay. What he had to say then evokes the qualities that were to make Impressionism a lasting and vital phenomenon. He pays particular attention to the Impressionists' capturing of the conditions of light, colour, and form as they are transmitted unmediated to the artist's eye at a particular moment in time:

> In a landscape bathed with light, in which entities are modelled as if in coloured *grisaille* [i.e. monochrome painting in greyish colour], the academic painter sees nothing but white light spreading everywhere, whilst the Impressionist sees it bathing everything, not in dead whiteness, but in a thousand conflicting vibrations, in rich prismatic decompositions of colour. Where

the academic sees only lines at the edge of things . . . the Impressionist sees real living lines, without geometrical form, built from thousands of irregular touches which, at a distance, give the thing life. Where the academic sees only things set down in regular, separate positions . . . the Impressionist sees perspective established by thousands of imperceptible tones and touches, by the variety of atmospheric states, with each plane not immobile, but shifting . . . The Impressionist sees and renders nature as she is, which is to say solely by means of coloured vibrations. Neither drawing, nor light, nor modelling, nor perspective, nor chiaroscuro: these infantile classifications all resolve in reality into coloured vibrations, and must be obtained on the canvas solely by coloured vibrations.

ART IN THE SECOND EMPIRE

Stop, monsieur le Président, here is France's shame.

JEAN-LÉON GÉRÔME TO PRÉSIDENT LOUBET, 1900

Pissarro, Manet, Degas, Sisley, Monet, Bazille, and Morisot were all born between 1830 and 1841 into a France whose recent history had been as dramatic and changeable as the era the painters were to live through. France had not had a history of durable regimes; by the end of 1830 the King, Charles X, had abdicated after the July revolution in Paris, to be replaced by the Duke of Orleans, Louis Philippe, who assumed the lieutenant-generalship of France. Louis Philippe devoted himself to the bourgeoisie and the *juste milieu,* but ironically ruled amidst periodic riot and revolt until 1848 when Paris once again erupted in revolution, causing the abdication of Louis Philippe and the

birth of the Second Republic. Two of the new republic's first acts were the Proclamation of Universal Suffrage and the Abolition of Slavery. In December 1848 Louis Napoleon, nephew of Napoleon I, was elected President of the Republic. Three years later, after the *coup d'état* of 1851, Louis Napoleon became Emperor Napoleon III. Napoleon III marked the start of his rule with a crack-down on political dissent and a suppression of the press while at the same time regulating the price of bread and encouraging growth in industry and commerce. France had languished behind the rest of Europe as the Industrial Revolution gained momentum, but Napoleon III's reign saw the development of banking institutions – the Credits Mobilier, Lyonnais, and Agricole – as well as railways and factories. As a patron of the arts, and of painting in particular, Napoleon III and his Arts Minister, Comte de Nieuwerkerke, were generous in reforming and developing a useful system of patronage, education and officially-commissioned works of art for public buildings.

In 1863 the Salon des Refusés, a massive exhibition of paintings which had been rejected by the Salon and for which Napoleon III bore great responsibility in many ways, marked the beginning of a new era of artistic freedom, even though it was a subtle attempt by the authorities to discredit critics of the official Salon. Not surprisingly, the Emperor's personal taste in painting favoured the academic style with its high finish and erudite classical and biblical subjects, although Romantics like Delacroix had little trouble making very successful careers for themselves under the Second Empire. However, a group of Realists who were more concerned with "common subjects", which had emerged under the vociferous leadership of Gustave Courbet, was anathema to Napoleon III's imperial sensibilities (as indeed were Courbet's socialist politics).

The new art, shortly to be named Impressionism, which succeeded Courbet, took as its subject matter not only nature, but also the prosperous middle class which had begun to make itself felt in the Second Empire. Edouard Manet's *Music in the Tuileries Gardens* (*Musique dans le Jardin des Tuileries*) of 1862 is regarded as one of the first great paintings of modern urban life, and what it shows is a bustling middle-class crowd of professionals and artists at their leisure. It is representative of a nation,

transformed in part by the policies of Napoleon III into an economically competitive state ready to enjoy its new found success and confidence.

To advance his nation further, Napoleon III had embarked on a series of successful wars against Austria, Russia, and China. In 1855 and 1867 the spectacular Expositions Universelles in Paris, rivalling the British Great Exhibition of 1851, announced to the nation and the world that France had arrived. Alas, the vagaries of French history caught up with Napoleon III. In 1870, just as he was attempting a measure of political liberalization, he seriously misjudged the nation's readiness for conflict and engaged in war against Prussia on a point of diplomatic etiquette. (The French were so convinced they could win this war they issued their officers with maps of Germany only!) Hopelessly out-organized, out-manouevred and out-gunned by the very artillery pieces which Krupps had exhibited to great acclaim in the 1867 Paris Exposition, the French armies disintegrated, with the loss of the important eastern province of Alsace-Lorraine. The Prussians invaded Paris in September 1870, and the Second Empire fell soon after.

After the Prussians had paraded through Paris and the new, broadly-republican government had attempted to disarm the National Guard there, the city erupted into revolution resulting in the Commune of 1871. Victor Hugo called it *l'année terrible*, a brief violent revolution which rose against the government and ended in massacre. In one week 20,000 Parisians were killed as civil war erupted in the streets of what had recently been *la ville lumière*, the dazzling capital of Europe. Scarcely two years before Monet's *Boulevard des*

PIERRE-AUGUSTE RENOIR
Self-portrait
c.1875.

Capucines went on show in 1873, the boulevards of Paris had been stripped of trees cut down for firewood; the animals in the zoos, including the elephants (but not the hippo, which no butcher could afford to buy), as well as the city's race-horses, had been slaughtered for food in the beseiged and starving city. Yet these momentous events touched the work of the Impressionists very little. There is no trace of upheaval in any of the Impressionists' paintings; most fled to avoid the war and only Manet and Degas remained in Paris. The former, who had been an anti-imperialist since the age of sixteen, was the only one amongst the group to record the bloody events of the Commune. But we shall see, the relationship of Manet and Degas with the other Impressionists is a special case in itself.

The Franco-Prussian war and the brief and bloody rise and fall of the Paris Commune formed the conclusion to the Second Empire. During the childhood and adolescence of the Impressionists many changes had swept over France, such as the massive construction of railways throughout the country to rival the systems of both Britain and the German states. Between 1851 and 1859 the French railways had trebled in length, facilitating the further expansion of industry and communications. Importantly for the Impressionists and their precursors who painted in the open air, the growth of the railways made the countryside available to the city-dweller in a way that was to have great consequences. During the Second Empire and well into the Third Republic, the cities, and Paris in particular, were undergoing fundamental change whilst in rural France the way of life was altered very little – only the occasional industrial chimney is to be

seen poking up in the background of the Impressionists' landscapes.

In 1853 Napoleon III had appointed Baron Georges-Eugène Haussmann, Prefect of the Seine, to set about the reconstruction of Paris. This he began with grandiloquent gusto, aiming to transform a city of narrow streets and congested, practically medieval areas – a city with a hopelessly inefficient transport and sanitation infrastructure, a city where the bourgeoisie lived cheek by jowl with the very poorest underclass – into a modern European capital. Haussmann built great sewers after the example of London, but for the removal of rainwater, not, unfortunately, for sewage, and gutted huge sections in the centre of the city to make way for broad boulevards with pavements, avenues of trees and clear sight-lines for the military – popular uprisings would thus be easier to control. Haussmann built eighty-five miles of new roads that included the rue de Rivoli and the boulevard Saint-Michel. Along these new roads, modern buildings quickly sprang up, their height and style controlled by the authorities. For more than a decade Paris was a wonderland of new buildings, roads, squares, and other construction projects.

The Impressionists found the transformed city and its *banlieues* (suburbs) an ideal place for a new and modern kind of art, a place which, according to writer Edmond de Goncourt, made one a "stranger . . . to these new boulevards with no turnings, no chance perspectives, implacably straight, which are no longer of Balzac's world, but which make one think of some American Babylon of the future." The Impressionists, in contrast, were not so much afraid as fascinated by the new lines of Paris. The mile-long perspectives

MARY CASSATT
Self-portrait
c.1895.

offered by the new boulevards, the St Lazare station in the centre and the railway bridges on the outskirts became the subjects, for example, of Monet's urban paintings.

What "Haussmannization" meant, above all, was the gentrification of Paris, making its centre the exclusive habitat of the bourgeoisie. However, behind these new streets the slums that had been cleared reappeared, only more cramped and squalid. Meanwhile hundreds of thousands of workers had been moved out to new industrial suburbs and slum areas, like Belleville and Ménilmontant, where they subsisted much as they had done before, but this time dispossessed of their ancient city.

When the rubble of 1870–71, caused by heavy Prussian bombardment and violent civil war, was cleared away, Paris quickly became *la ville lumière* it had been during the Second Empire. By 1874 it was hard to imagine that dogs and rats had once been on the menu. Although memories of the civil war remained, the economic growth of the Second Empire resumed under a republican guise. Paris reclaimed its place as the centre of European art.

The Impressionists lived in an age of struggle between modernity and a traditional order. We see in their paintings a radical, and, for their time, shocking break with traditional notions of art, the culmination, but not the end, of a series of new ways of seeing. The Abstract movement of the twentieth century stemmed from experiments with existing art just as the Impressionists' innovations grew out of the paintings of Courbet, Corot, Delacroix, Constable, and the old masters who had gone before in the world of art.

We are surrounded by the art of the Impressionists – the legacy of a relatively brief period in the history of art which has endured in the most diverse of ways. There is scarcely a wall, a mug, a postcard, a jigsaw puzzle or indeed a box of chocolates which has not borne a reproduction of Degas' prima ballerinas, Manet's barmaid, Renoir's girl on a swing or one of Monet's haystacks. These images are perennial because they are windows on a bygone age of leisurely Parisian summers and intensely perceived light which appeal to us in this beleaguered post-modern century. They are also the masterpieces of a crucial period of change and works of art from an optimistic time of endless possibilities. The Impressionists' sense of wonderment at their world has, ironically, become for us a comforting reflection of times passed. Although it would be convenient to think that before Monet, Renoir, Sisley, and Pissarro light could never have been seen and set down in a series of broken, prismatic colours, that shadows were never blue or red, yet in fact these approaches were already becoming possible in the early nineteenth century. It is certainly true, nevertheless, that a short time after these artists had come together, blue shadows and green skies were, and have remained, commonplaces in the vocabulary of art.

The Impressionists were named in jest by a hostile critic; collectively they never published a manifesto – their name is a catch-all for a fragile movement of men and women briefly united in their belief that the time had come for a new art to be seen and appreciated. They came from different social backgrounds, from the patricians Manet and Degas to the working-class Renoir, and

EDGAR DEGAS
Self-portrait
c.1855.

MANET
Berthe Morisot
c.1869.

in the end their friendships broke up and they scattered across France. All of them, however, were in Paris during a critical period in French history; they knew and worked with each other and often lived in each other's pockets. Some – Monet, Sisley, and Pissarro, for example – were overwhelmingly attracted by the landscape and were driven to depict it. Others – Degas, Manet, and Renoir – were more concerned with the human figure and the life of the city and its suburbs. In their time they were all accused of being revolutionary; their supporters held them up as the iconographers of a new, modern age; their critics claimed they were subverting a set of artistic ideals and methods which had obtained for centuries.

In some ways the Impressionists were revolutionaries – in their use of colour, for example, or choice of subject and methods of exhibition, and in their assertion of the right to recreate the world as they saw it. The history of the Impressionists is full of contradictions. Edouard Manet (who together with Degas we should be wary of calling an Impressionist in any case), a generous and devoted supporter of the younger artists such as Monet, Renoir, and Sisley, never exhibited in the series of Impressionist exhibitions which shook the Parisian art world. However, he had caused a sensation a decade before with *Luncheon on the Grass* (*Déjeuner sur l'herbe*), and though he was considered to be their leader, he sought distinction through the Salon – a reluctant revolutionary. Degas, of the same generation as Manet, exhibited in all eight of the Impressionists' shows from 1874 to 1886. Monet, Renoir, and Sisley all dropped out of the group's exhibitions in the late 1870s, whilst the most politically revolutionary of them all,

Pissarro, would not abandon Degas (politically an arch-Conservative and anti-Semite) or the Impressionist exhibitions even when the others begged him to. Despite all of these contradictions there existed for a short period in late nineteenth-century France a movement, a loose and informal "academy" whose members learned from one another and changed the course of art.

When Claude Monet died in 1926, Impressionism was firmly enshrined in the past – new forces had been at work since the 1880s. In the lifetime of Monet and most of the Impressionists France had seen two revolutions, the rise and fall of the Second Empire and the establishment of the Third Republic. An industrial revolution had taken place and Paris had been rebuilt almost from scratch. The Impressionists' own revolution was intimately tied up with that of the world they inhabited. Innovations as seemingly mundane as the mass manufacture of oil paint in tin tubes and the portable easel had freed the artist from his or her studio. Monet's *Boulevard des Capucines* was painted from the window of Nadar's studio high up in the same boulevard, introducing literally a new angle on traditional views of Paris.

By the last years of the nineteenth century the Impressionist style had spread and prospered, evolving into Neo- and Post-Impressionism. But the shock waves of Impressionism continued to reverberate. In 1900, over a quarter of a century after the first Impressionist exhibition, the academician Gérôme, one of the most successful artists of his century, was guiding Président Loubet of France around the Exposition Universelle when he stopped him at the entrance to the Impressionist Room with these words: *"Arrêtez, monsieur le Président, c'est ici le déshonneur de la France!"*

MONET
The Artist's Garden at Argenteuil
oil on canvas
1872. 61 × 74cm (24 × 29in)

THE BIRTH OF
IMPRESSIONISM

SEVERAL INFLUENCES IN THE earlier part of the nineteenth
century are crucial to the development of Impressionism.
In the first three decades of the century the inspiration
of Dutch and English landscapists began to have an important
effect on French landscape painting and art in general. Eugène
Delacroix – who was to influence many of the Impressionists,
especially Renoir – had brought a new brilliance of colour and
virtuosity of brushwork to his paintings of exotic subjects
and was a keen admirer of Constable, as were the Barbizon
School of *plein-air*, or open-air, painters attempting a new
naturalism in and around the Fontainebleau Forest. The latter
were the precursors of Monet and Pissarro, who were also
deeply influenced by the landscapists Eugène Boudin and
Johan Jongkind working on the Normandy coast. By mid-
century the Realists had come to prominence headed by
Gustave Courbet, who had rejected the fanciful nature of
Delacroix's Romanticism and was painting down-to-earth
contemporary and allegorical subjects. All of these trends were
significant in creating a world of art where Impressionism
could flourish.

In 1863 the Salon was so oversubscribed that an exhibition of
the thousands of rejected works was mounted after a popular
outcry. Edouard Manet caused a scandal with his *Luncheon on the
Grass* which portrayed its classical subject in a modern idiom to
shocking effect and he became the reluctant leader of the
younger generation of Monet, Renoir, Sisley, and Bazille who
had come together the year before at the atelier of Charles
Gleyre and formed the nucleus of the Impressionists.

COROT
Landscape at
Mornex, Savoy
(DETAIL) oil on
canvas Undated.
40 × 61.5cm
(16 × 24in)

1820–1863: From the English Landscape
to the Salon des Refusés

*. . . I did not really see a less negative colour, but I felt as if
it were an effort towards a less negative colour, the pulsation
of a hesitant ray struggling to discharge its light.*

Marcel Proust, *Swann's Way*

The Impressionists *par excellence*, Monet, Pissarro, Sisley, and Renoir, met in Paris in the early 1860s and were bound together in their admiration for the work of an older generation of landscape painters who had left their studios to paint in the open air in the countryside near Paris. Tracing the immediate origins of Impressionism, a phenomenon which began in the French countryside, takes us back to the English landscape and the excitement felt by early nineteenth-century French Romantic painters, such as Eugène Delacroix and Théodore Géricault, on encountering the experiments and achievements in oil and watercolour of the English landscape painters John Constable, J.M.W. Turner, and Richard Bonington.

In 1820 the French writer Charles Nodier, whose drawing room in Paris was an important place for the dissemination of news and ideas in the arts, was in London at the Royal Academy summer exhibition. In Nodier's journal, entitled *From Dieppe to the Mountains of Scotland*, he offered the following opinion of the summer exhibition:

In painting, landscapes and sea views are the pieces in which the English have the fewest rivals in Europe . . . the palm of the exhibition belongs to a large landscape by Constable to which the ancient or modern masters have very few masterpieces that could be put in opposition. Near, it is only broad daubings of ill-laid colour which offend the touch as well as the sight, they are so coarse and uneven. At the distance of a few steps it is picturesque country, rustic dwellings, a low river where little waves foam over the pebbles, a cart crossing a pond. It is water, air and sky . . .

When Eugène Delacroix saw *The Hay Wain* at the Paris Salon of 1824 he was so impressed by the natural transparency and brilliance of colour in Constable's sky, trees, earth, and water that he immediately set about reworking his own *Massacre at Chois* (*Massacre à Scio*), a painting which he had almost finished, adding glaze and thick patches of pure pigment in various colours in an attempt to emulate the effect of the Englishman's work. Delacroix's radical use of colour and his technique of *flochetage*, using large flakes (*floches*) of colour to heighten his forms, was later to be developed further by the Impressionists.

Théodore Géricault, a fellow Romantic of Delacroix's, had seen *The Hay Wain* in London, two years

BONINGTON
The Large Pond, Palace of Versailles oil on canvas c.1820.
43.5 × 54.5cm (17 × 22in)
ABOVE Avoiding the popular aspects of Versailles, Bonington indicates the obvious touristic elements of the scene as sketchy masses in the background. Everything here is subordinated to the depiction of space and volume.

before Delacroix's encounter with it at the 1824 Salon, and had expressed his astonishment to Delacroix and others on his return to Paris. With the enthusiasm of Nodier, the shock experienced by the critic Délécluze, who admitted that in comparison to *The Hay Wain* French landscape painting of the 1820s was "heavy, insensitive, and false", and the practical interest of Delacroix and Géricault in the English landscapists' work, an important step had been taken along the road which was eventually to lead to Monet and Pissarro.

During the 1820s and 1830s the sketches of Constable, Turner, and Bonington were of particular interest to Delacroix and his contemporaries. In order to capture "with a pure apprehension of natural effect," the incessantly changing qualities of light and colour, Delacroix observed that in the natural world "light and shadow never stand still." Consequently, the French Romantic painters developed the habit of making quick, but by no means cursory, sketches of a particular scene in oil and watercolour. These sketches, although they were not considered

CONSTABLE
A Cottage among Trees with a Sand Bank
oil on paper on canvas c.1830.
18 × 22cm (7 × 9in)
BELOW An example of Constable's direct approach to landscape. The sketchy nature of works such as this was particularly influential in France.

to be "finished" by the authorities and Salons of the time, are of importance in the development both of the artist's way of seeing the world and the technique of depicting it. They display to a remarkable degree the totality of the artist's vision and observation, and are nowadays often more highly prized than the "finished" work they frequently preceded. In fact, Delacroix and many others of his generation agreed that the vitality of outdoor sketches suffered from being transferred and reworked into studio compositions.

Until Constable and his fellow English landscapists had made their dazzling impact on the French art establishment in the 1820s, French landscape painting had enjoyed an honourable, if dull history. It is often, though quite wrongly, assumed that the Académie in Paris at this time had no interest in the promotion of landscape painting. A major quadrennial competition in historical landscape painting, the Prix de Paysage Historique, had been instigated at the Ecole des Beaux-Arts in 1817 after many years of agitation by landscapists for the genre to be recognized within the school's establishment. Although the competition for the Prix de Paysage Historique was abolished in 1863 – a date central to the history of Impressionism as it marked the first Salon des Refusés – the teaching of landscape painting at the Ecole was at a significant level of development by the time Constable showed *The Hay Wain* at the 1824 Salon in Paris.

It is important to note that the Prix de Paysage Historique was

precisely that – a competition for historical landscape, not landscape after nature or *paysage champêtre*. To compete, students had to choose a classical or biblical theme "of the noble and historical type" for their subject, and figures to be set in the landscape were not to exceed a prescribed height and disturb the proportions of a picture which was, after all, to be devoted to landscape. Despite this, the teaching of landscape after nature at the Ecole was surprisingly advanced, echoing some of the dicta of Constable and vaguely foreshadowing the loose theories of the Impressionists. J.B. Deperthes, who published his *Théorie de paysage* (*Landscape Theory*) in 1818, advised students of landscape painting that their aim in depicting nature was to paint it "in the light that falls on it at the exact moment when the painter sets out to capture the scene." According to the landscapist Pierre-Henri Valenciennes (who was partly responsible for the Prix de Paysage Historique), under whom Deperthes had studied, a study (*étude*) for a landscape painting made "from Nature should be done within two hours at the outside,

CONSTABLE

The Hay Wain oil on canvas 1821.
130 × 185.5cm
(51 × 73in)
The quintessential English landscape, admired by Delacroix and Géricault for its dramatic naturalism. Delacroix reworked his own painting The Massacre at Chios *after he had seen Constable's great landscape at the Salon of 1824. This and other works by the English landscapists were a source of inspiration to the Barbizon School and their successors, the Impressionists.*

and if your effect is a sunrise or a sunset, you should not take more than half an hour." Neither of these two instructions would have been out of place in a hypothetical manual of the art of Impressionism. Yet landscape painters such as Constable, Bonington, Valenciennes, and Deperthes were confined by tradition to their studios for the completion of their works of art. Painting outdoors did not lead to acceptably "finished" pieces of art. Indeed, Constable, as he was working in his London studio on *The Hay Wain*, was forced to dispatch an underling to the depths of East Anglia to make drawings of the eponymous cart. After the apprentice returned with the drawing Constable then completed the composition of the picture. This was the most practical approach.

The move into the country and the development of the idea that a sketch made outdoors, *en plein air*, was a legitimate end in itself came with a group of painters known as the Barbizon School. Barbizon is a village in the Fontainebleau Forest to the southeast of Paris. The Fontainebleau Forest and the nearby plain of Chailly had been locations for painters since the mid-eighteenth century, and had been suggested by Valenciennes as useful substitutes for the Roman

COURBET
Entrance to the Straits of Gibraltar
oil on canvas 1848.
18 × 26cm (7 × 10in)
Small, hastily executed sketches were not made for public consumption, but the aesthetic of the sketch or study was gaining ground amongst French landscapists in the mid-nineteenth century.

Campagna, a landscape held in great esteem for its classical associations. Between 1830 and 1850 a group of landscape painters, which included Constant Troyon, Théodore Rousseau, Virgile Diaz de la Peña, François Daubigny, François Millet, and Jean-Baptiste Corot, made use of the area around Barbizon and often settled there for long periods. Daubigny was a devoted *plein-air* painter who built a studio boat in order to paint *in situ* on the river Oise (an example later followed by Monet). In 1891 Frédéric Henriet, in his biography *The Campaigns of a Landscape Painter* (*Les Campagnes d'un paysagiste*), describes Daubigny's struggle with the elements:

> Daubigny attached his canvas to some posts solidly planted in the ground. And there it stayed, continually exposed to the horns of cattle and the pranks of naughty children until it was completely finished. The painter had specifically chosen a turbulent sky filled with large clouds chased by the angry wind. He was constantly on the alert for the right moment and ran to take up his work as soon as the weather corresponded to that of his painting.

The Barbizon School was as indebted to the English landscapists as Delacroix although in historical

DAUBIGNY
Spring
oil on canvas 1857.
96 × 193cm (38 × 76in)
A perfect example of the Barbizon landscape, Daubigny's painting was exhibited at the Salon of 1857 which was transferred that year from the Salon D'Apollon in the Louvre to the larger Palais de l'Industrie.

terms the art being created around Barbizon quickly came to represent a strong reaction against the Romanticism of Delacroix and Géricault, who were not particularly interested in landscape or *plein-airisme* as a genre or method of painting. Just as the Romantics had rebelled against the ingrained Neo-Classicism of the Académie, as exemplified by David and Ingres and taught in the Ecole des Beaux-Arts, so the painting of nature for its own sake amounted to a rejection of both the erudite Neo-Classical and the flamboyant Romantic subject matter. The Barbizon painters, as well as admiring the English landscapists of their own era, were much taken with the eminent seventeenth-century Dutch School of landscape painting, particularly the works of Ruysdael and Hobbema. In this the Barbizon School was supported by the Director of the Académie, Théophile Thoré, who had commissioned Rousseau and made an extensive study of Dutch art. On the other hand the Comte de Nieuwerkerke, the Director-General of National Museums after 1849, spoke for many when he

MILLET
The Potato Harvest
oil on canvas
1858. 54 × 65cm
(21 × 26in)
The dignity of peasant labour was Millet's great, if somewhat sentimental, theme. Pissaro, and later van Gogh, were influenced by Millet's depictions of the arduous life of the peasant. Millet's work did not find favour with the establishment which preferred idealized landscapes and peasants.

described the Barbizon School in the following incandescent and patronizing terms: "This is the painting of democrats, of those who don't change their linen and who want to put themselves above men of the world. This art displeases and disquiets me."

Thankfully the Comte de Nieuwerkerke and the French authorities were increasingly disquietened to find their stranglehold on matters of taste weakening. The clear line of development from the Dutch to the English artists, and thence the French landscape painters and their attempt to capture "the exact moment", was leading to the art of Monet and his fellow Impressionists.

Capturing the landscape meant being in it, with all the attendant dangers and inconvenience of being away from the controlled environment of the studio. In 1841 John Goffe Rand, an American portraitist living in London, had invented the first collapsible paint tube, an idea quickly taken up by the colour merchants Winsor and Newton. As Pierre-Auguste Renoir is reported by his son Jean to have said, "Without paints in tubes there would have been no Cézanne, no Monet, no Sisley or Pissarro, nothing of what the journalists were later to call Impressionism."

Before the arrival of these new tubes, made of inert tin so as not to react with the various chemicals in the pigment, the ground pigment was supplied by the colour merchant, mixed with oil by the painter and kept in a small pouch of pig's bladder. To use the paint, the artist had to make a small hole in the wall of the bladder and squeeze it out. For centuries these bladders had been the only way of dispensing a ready mixed combination of pigment and oil, but paint could not be kept for long in them before the oil began to oxidize. Once opened, the life of the paint – made up of expensive pigments – was considerably shortened. The tin tube was a revolutionary device by comparison, both for the colour merchant, who had a new product with which to service an increasing clientèle of amateur or "Sunday" painters littering the banks of the Seine on summer days, and the serious artist, who could now venture outdoors confident that the paint was in a stable condition and swiftly to hand. The tube paint had the consistency of fresh butter, which made it ideal for application to the canvas in thick impasto brushstrokes, or even with the palette knife – both methods used by the Impressionists and after them to particularly remarkable effect by Vincent van Gogh. The paint could still of course be further tempered with linseed, walnut, or poppy oil, or diluted with turpentine.

To fill the new tubes a whole new range of bright, stable colours with well-understood drying properties began to appear on the market. The advancement of mineral and organic chemistry in the early part of the century had heralded new colours such as cobalt blue, artificial ultramarine (previously made of lapis lazuli, very expensive and available only in small quantities), chromium yellow with its shades of orange, red and green, emerald green, zinc white and a stable lead white. By the 1850s the artist had at his or her disposal a palette more brilliant, stable and convenient than ever before.

In 1839 the French chemist Eugène Chevreul, director of dyeing at the Gobelins tapestry workshop, who had begun an investigation into why some dyed colours seemed less brilliant than others, published his study *On the Law of Simultaneous Colour Contrast and the Arrangement of Coloured Objects* (better known as *The Principles of Harmony and Contrast of Colours*), which explained the phenomenon that when two

The four pictures here have been enlarged to show the details of the brushwork of the four master Impressionists – Manet, Pissarro, Monet, and Renoir. The essential similarity between them, and the obvious comparison to be made with the refined, concentrated brushwork of the classical schools and the conventional artists of the time, is the looseness and immediacy of the strokes.

MANET
An Italian Woman
oil on canvas
Private collection

PISSARRO
ABOVE The Farmyard
oil on canvas 1877.
55 × 65cm (22 × 26in)

colours are placed touching one another the differences between them are perceived to be at their greatest. From this he codified a theory of colours which says that certain pairs of colours, such as green and red, or violet and yellow, complement each other. This gives rise to the phenomenon of "negative or complementary after-image" where the complementary colour of a red, i.e. green, can be seen as an aura around the colour when staring at the red for a moment and then looking away. As the German poet and scientist Johan Wolfgang von Goethe had already observed in his *Theory of Colours* written in 1810, a deep red sunset produced the complementary colour of green in

RENOIR
ABOVE The White Hat oil on canvas 1890. 55.5 × 46cm (22 × 18in)

MONET
BELOW The Red Road oil on canvas 1884. 65 × 81cm (26 × 32in)

MILLET
Bringing Home the New-born Calf
oil on canvas
1857–61. 81 × 99cm (32 × 39in)
ABOVE Like The Potato Harvest,
*this painting was ridiculed by some
contemporary critics, who considered
Millet's subjects to be vulgar and
unworthy of fine art.*

the shadows cast by the sunlight;
likewise, the yellowish tinge of
snow produced shadows of a violet
hue. Delacroix had used coloured
shadow in his work, and the
Impressionists were to exploit their
own perception and Chevreul's
theory further with the bright
new colours available to them,
whilst the Neo-Impressionists were
to take this phenomenon to its
logical extreme.

Meanwhile, the Realism
developed by François Millet and
Gustave Courbet, which was a
complete rejection of Neo-Classical
and Romantic styles, began, in the
late 1850s and early 1860s, to have
a strong influence on young
painters like Monet. Millet's great
achievement was to paint the
peasantry as he found and
remembered it, being himself the
son of a Normandy peasant farmer.

Although paintings such as *The Gleaners* (*Les Glaneurs*) and *Angélus* show the peasantry at back-breaking work and pious rest, and do not appear today to be particularly realistic, their very subject matter was a cause for fierce controversy at the time among those traditionalists who thought agricultural labour a subject unfit for "proper" representation, and those at the other extreme who believed Millet's work to be the embodiment of socialist values. Despite the claims of the right and the left, Millet remained resolutely apolitical.

Not so Gustave Courbet, the son of a wealthy wine grower from Ornans near Switzerland. Courbet's art, like his politics, was uncompromising. His choice of subjects eschewed everything that had previously been thought suitable for fine art. They were, as Bernard Denvir observes, "unheroic, unhistorical, and entirely unconcerned either with religious symbolism or patriotic propaganda." Courbet was a friend and *comrade* of the printer Pierre Joseph Proudhon, the title of whose work of 1850 *What is Property?* (*Qu'est-ce que la propriété?*) was answered with the immortal words: "It is theft" (*"C'est le vol"*). Courbet's staunch socialism ensured him a spectacular career in politics, eventually landing him in jail for taking part in the destruction of the

COURBET
A Spanish Woman
oil on canvas
1855. 81 × 65cm (32 × 26in)
As usual, Courbet does not try to prettify his sitters.

COURBET
The Burial at Ornans
oil on canvas
1849–50. 315 × 668cm
(124 × 263in)
*ABOVE Courbet received a medal at
the Salon in 1850, but not for this
painting. The massive, dark,
unconventional composition showing
the lower echelons of society provoked
outraged criticism. Courbet's Realism
was deeply influenced by the political
ideas of Pierre Joseph Proudhon, of
whom he was a supporter. Courbet's
rejection of historical and religious
subjects made him a champion of
the new generation of the "painters
of modern life".*

COURBET
The Artist's Studio
oil on canvas 1855.
360 × 600cm (142 × 236in)
*OPPOSITE This painting is subtitled an
"Allegory of Realism", and the artist has
indeed filled his picture with symbols
and contemporary figures. Right, seated
on the table: the poet Baudelaire. Right
centre: Champfleury. Right, third from
left: another friend of Courbet's, the
socialist writer Proudhon. In the shadow
to the left, seated in profile: the barely
disguised figure of Napoleon III, much
disliked by Courbet and his radical
friends. Left, seated, wearing a top hat:
a right-wing journalist. Standing, left: a
figure identified as the banker Fould.*

*The woman nursing a child is Irish; she
represents poverty and destitution. The
dummy behind the easel has been
symbolically discarded in favour of a
real woman.*

Vendôme Column, a huge victory memorial in the heart of Paris. But in spite of his radicalism in painting and politics he exhibited two works, *The Stone Breakers* (*Les Casseurs de pierre*) and *The Burial at Ornans*, at the Salon of 1850. "I hold", Courbet wrote in 1861, "that painting is essentially a concrete art and does not consist of anything but the representation of real and concrete things". Five years later, at the Exposition Universelle in Paris, Courbet erected his own Realist Pavilion (Pavillon du Réalisme) where he rivalled the official Salon by showing forty pictures including the massive *The Artist's Studio* (*L'Atelier du peintre*), which depicts in "an Allegory of Realism" the artist and the influences at work on him.

In the decade after 1850 French painting underwent an unparalleled fragmentation of styles, partly tolerated but never promoted by the authorities. The experiments of the Barbizon School and the Realists were encouraging the young painters who had been born in the 1830s and 1840s along a path which was artistically a logical progression but which was to appear to the public and the arbiters of the Salon shockingly revolutionary. By the time the Impressionists began to show in the mid-1870s, the Barbizon artists were readily accepted by the Salon and their work was beginning to fetch high prices.

PISSARRO, MANET AND DEGAS

Camille Pissarro, Edouard Manet, and Edgar Degas, born in 1830, 1832, and 1834 respectively, were in their twenties when the 1855 Exposition Universelle was proving to be the delight of Paris. The work of Delacroix, who was now fifty-seven and achieving great popular acclaim, was the main attraction, having been eloquently lauded by the poet and art critic Charles Baudelaire (who was later to befriend Manet). Work by Daubigny, Corot, and Millet was also to be seen hidden amongst the thousands of paintings on show, but it would have been difficult to miss Courbet's spectacular sideshow.

Pissarro, the third son of Franco-Jewish parents, had arrived in Paris from St Thomas, a Danish colony in the Virgin Islands where his father was a merchant. Camille had been to school in France, but after returning to St Thomas to work in his father's store, he had gone to Venezuela in 1853 to work with the Danish artist Fritz Melbye. Eventually his parents decided to send him to Paris to study art. He

arrived in 1855, as the Exposition was in progress, to attend the Ecole des Beaux-Arts. He soon left the Ecole for the Académie Suisse, a studio in the quai des Orfèvres, run by an ex-model, which charged small fees, offered no teaching, but had models and equipment for young artists to use as they wished. At the Exposition Universelle, Pissarro was particularly impressed by the six Corots on show – the young Pissarro had become a landscapist under the influence of his friend Melbye and later went to visit Corot in search of guidance. A couple of years later he was found by Claude Monet to be "peacefully working away in Corot's style"; ten years after the Exposition Universelle, Pissarro was officially exhibiting at the Salon as Corot's pupil. At that time it would be hard to imagine that he would become, with the exception of Claude Monet, perhaps the most influential of the landscape Impressionists.

In contrast to Camille Pissarro, Edouard Manet, twenty-three at the time of the Exposition, was the son of a Parisian magistrate, a member of the *haute bourgeoisie* and blessed, as was his slightly younger contemporary Edgar Degas, with the security of independent means. He had enrolled in the school of Thomas Couture in 1850, where he studied painting for six years. Couture had been a pupil of Paul Delaroche, whose *The Execution of Lady Jane Grey* exemplified the conservative but popular qualities of the Davidian academic style. The painting had delighted the Salon of 1834 where visitors are reported to

COROT
The Forest of Fontainebleau
oil on canvas
c.1855. 39 × 54.5cm (15 × 22in)
The archetypal Barbizon landscape.

have wept. They were no doubt moved by the sight of the young English noblewoman with her head on the block, a fate close to the hearts of all French citizens not so long after the mass executions that followed the 1789 Revolution.

Couture had caused controversy and ensured himself his own place in the popular imagination of the French public and critics with his huge painting *The Romans of the Decadence* (*Les Romains de la décadence*), a sprawling depiction of a Roman orgy which shocked and titillated Parisian society when it was shown at the Salon of 1847. In the same year, doubtless to make the most of his new-found notoriety, Couture had opened his own private art school in Paris, advertising it as offering "teaching based above all on the great art of ancient Greece, the Renaissance masters and the admirable Flemish school." Couture, in order to clarify his view further, declared himself against the "spurious classical school which reproduces the works of the past in a banal and imperfect fashion," and "hostile to that abominable school, known [as] Romantic."

All this was true to the spirit of Louis Philippe's *juste milieu*, and linked Couture to his contemporaries such as Charles Gleyre and Alexander Cabanel, who were in fact content to use

COUTURE
The Romans of the Decadence
oil on canvas 1847.
466 × 775cm (184 × 305in)
Couture, the teacher of Manet, scored an immense success with this work at the Salon of 1847.

those elements of Classicism, Romanticism and even Realism which would make up an acceptable picture. As an allegory of contemporary hedonism veiled in the skimpy tunic of Classicism, *The Romans of the Decadence* stands in ironic contrast to the *juste milieu* professed by all and which was to continue after the fall of Louis Philippe and well into the Third Republic. The burgeoning French middle classes of the 1850s would have been outraged if Couture had depicted the contemporary French male bourgeoisie at one of its favourite leisure activities, the brothel. Yet, this is exactly what Couture's pupil Edouard Manet set out to do eight years later at the Salon des Refusés of 1863 with his *Luncheon on the Grass* (*Déjeuner sur l'herbe*). That painting scandalized Paris and pushed Manet reluctantly into the forefront of what became the Impressionist movement.

During his time as a young "apprentice" at Couture's atelier Manet was less concerned with shocking Paris than studying his master's teaching and pondering how literally to reverse the academic technique to his own ends. He also spent many hours in the Louvre studying and copying the techniques of the old masters. The Spanish artists Velazquez, Murillo, and Ribera particularly

MANET
Copy after Delacroix's Dante
oil on canvas
1855. 33 × 41cm (13 × 16in)
Manet went to see the deeply respected Delacroix with his friend Antonin Proust, and asked permission to copy his work.

DEGAS
Self-portrait
oil on canvas
1854–55. 81 × 64.5cm
(32 × 25in)
One of many self-portraits the artist painted in his youth.

interested him; an influence which can be seen in his later paintings. During his time spent copying in the Louvre he also absorbed elements of a number of other masters including the French Le Nain brothers. Manet was in effect a pivotal force in the long tradition of European art. His wish was to evolve from the old masters, not reject what he had learned from them. He was also significantly in awe of Delacroix, so much so that in 1855 he wrote to him asking permission to copy his *Barque of Dante* (*La Barque de Dante*).

Edgar Degas was the youngest of his generation of artists to study in Paris in the mid-1850s. He spent only one semester at the Ecole des Beaux-Arts, however, before an extended tour of Italy where part of his family lived. Degas was the son of Franco-Italian parents who had made their fortune in banking. He registered with the painting and sculpture section of the Ecole des Beaux-Arts on 6th April 1855 after passing an entrance competition at which the painter Henri Fantin-Latour was also successful. (Fantin-Latour, however, was found wanting and left three months later.) Degas' teacher during his brief studies at the Ecole was Louis Lamothe, who inspired him with his own deeply held respect for Ingres, whose pictures in any case Degas had been copying in the Louvre and at the homes of wealthy family friends for some time. In 1856 Degas was in Naples visiting his relatives, painting their portraits and touring the great museums of other Italian cities, absorbing all the Renaissance masters he could

feast his eyes on. Although he was to be a prime mover in the *Société anonyme* just under a decade later, the relationship of Degas' work to the other Impressionists was to be marked both by his experiences in Italy and by his abiding interest in the human form as opposed to the landscape.

THE NURSERY OF IMPRESSIONISM

In 1862 France annexed Cambodia, Victor Hugo published *Les Misérables*, Edouard Manet painted *Music in the Tuileries Gardens* and four unknown young artists met in the Paris atelier of Charles Gleyre, a fifty-four-year-old Swiss artist who had been an instructor at the Ecole des Beaux-Arts. Claude Monet, the eldest son of a grain merchant in the northwestern port of Le Hâvre, Frédéric Bazille, whose family were affluent wine producers in the southern Hérault, Auguste Renoir, previously a porcelain-painter, and Alfred Sisley, at twenty-three the oldest in the group by two years and the son of an English businessman, had little in common except art. Gleyre's atelier had a reputation for being cheap and Gleyre himself was known to be fairly tolerant and kind to his *élèves* (pupils). Although he was neither famous nor a member of the Académie, one painting by him, *Lost Illusions* of 1843, had enjoyed great success at the Salon. The painting won him a medal and substantial respect from the critics of the day.

The teachers of the Impressionists were men raised in

an academic ethos of painting which stretched back to principles laid down in the seventeenth century. To prepare for entry into the Ecole, aspiring artists in the mid-nineteenth century entrusted themselves (and their purses) to men such as Charles Gleyre and Thomas Couture who ran private independent ateliers where they could receive formal instruction (a system which persists to this day in France). Life at the atelier for a young *rapin*, or new boy, was often fraught with dangers. According to Albert Boime, the eminent historian of the Académie in the nineteenth century, the *rapin* would be first to arrive at the atelier in the morning and busied himself with menial tasks such as arranging the stools, sweeping the floor, washing the brushes, running errands and suffering occasional persecution by the older students. There were frequently initiation ceremonies, or *blagues*, for the hapless *rapins* to endure before they progressed in the social hierarchy of the atelier.

The course of studies pursued at the ateliers relied on a long tradition of ensuring that the student could draw proficiently before he could be allowed to touch a paintbrush. Drawing exercises which started with copying from engravings, then plaster casts of antique sculpture and finally the live models were rigorous and frequently mindnumbing. Only when the student had mastered drawing technique to a high degree would he be allowed to paint copies of the teacher's work or old masters in the Louvre, as did Manet, Degas and a reluctant Monet.

INGRES
The Princess of Broglie
oil on canvas
1853. 114.5 × 86cm
(45 × 34in)
Degas was a thorough draftsman and Ingres' perfection was an abiding model for him.

DEGAS
The Bellelli Family
oil on canvas
1858–60. 200 × 250cm
(79 × 98in)
Degas started a series of portraits while visiting his relatives in Italy.

An equally rigorous system of painting was taught in the ateliers and the Ecole with varying nuances of emphasis according to the predilection of the master. The practical work of painting on to the canvas was as strictly taught as drawing. The student was guided towards producing a painting of a nude or model's head known as an *académie*, which displayed the classical technique of applying the oil paint to the canvas in layers of tones from dark to light. These *académies* were often undertaken in shades of grey or with a very limited palette to produce flesh-tones, for colour was considered a distraction, the sort of thing Delacroix was considered too free with by teachers, yet whose pupils revelled in it. The smoothness in texture and gradation of tone in the finished *académie* was of prime importance. Yet however stifling this kind of training might have been, it had served Degas and Manet well.

So in 1862, the young Monet and his friends found themselves sitting on their stools in Gleyre's atelier, perhaps sketching a plaster copy of an antique statue as countless young art students had done before them. For Monet, the atelier must have been stuffy indeed. He stayed there for only eighteen months until Gleyre was forced to close, and afterwards attended the Académie Suisse. Monet was the son of a small businessman who had moved his family from Paris to Le Hâvre on the Normandy coast. The sea and the countryside of his youth were to become Claude Monet's natural habitat, not the Louvre or a Parisian atelier, and later years would find him braving the most appalling weather and terrain to capture a scene. He had returned to Paris on the sufferance of his father to study in the traditional way. Monet's artistic talents had already made an impact in Le Hâvre where he had been earning a reasonable living from selling caricatures. There he had met Eugène Boudin, a self-taught local landscapist, who persuaded him (initially reluctant, according to Monet) to take up painting in the open air. Of the four *rapins,* Monet was the most experienced in painting and with the new Realist philosophies – as exemplified in Courbet's paintings of "common" life – being thrown up around it. By the time he had gone to study with Gleyre he had already spent some time in Paris, done his military service in the

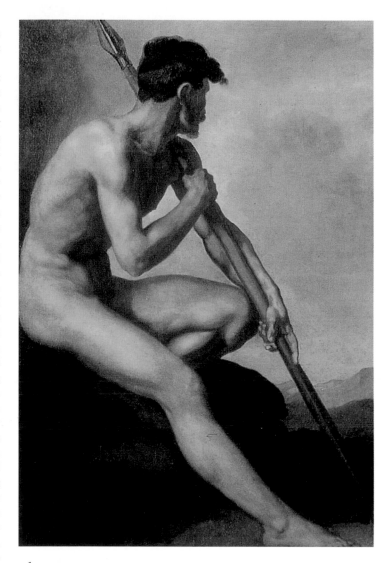

GÉRICAULT
Nude Warrior with a Spear
oil on canvas
1810. 93.5 × 75.5cm (37 × 30in)
Though it was painted half a century earlier, this type of academic nude was still taught with the same rigor at the Ecole des Beaux-Arts and the independent ateliers such as those of Gleyre and Couture.

MONET
Honfleur, rue de la Bavolle
oil on canvas
1864. 56 × 61cm (22 × 24in)
*The free rendering is reminiscent
of Corot's studies.*

French colony of Algeria and had been a habitué of the Brasserie des Martyrs at 75 rue des Martyrs, where Courbet, the art critic Jules Castagnary (who was to be a powerful spokesman for impressionism), Baudelaire, and François Bonvin (a conventional painter with advanced views) would meet, talk, and drink. Edouard Manet's work was much discussed there even though he himself was an infrequent visitor, preferring to hold court in other cafés.

Auguste Renoir's family were provincial tailors from Limoges who had moved to Paris shortly after he was born. He was apprenticed to a porcelain-painter (who went out of business in 1858) and then, for a living, Renoir painted fans, copying scenes from artists such as Fragonard, Watteau, and Boucher as well as painting blinds and other odd jobs before enrolling in Gleyre's atelier in 1861. Having been trained as an artistic craftsman, his whole philosophy in art was geared to the acquisition of technique. Like Manet and Degas, Renoir had studied the old masters in the Louvre, something Monet was reluctant to do. As the art historian John House has observed, by deciding to become a painter

Renoir was moving from a trade to a profession, from the skilled working class into the middle class, yet from the very beginning he seems consistently to have thought of himself as a workman in paint, an "*ouvrier de la peinture*". Unlike Renoir, who in the mid-1850s had been painting to live, Alfred Sisley and Frédéric Bazille had been living to paint. Sisley had narrowly avoided a business career in London and Bazille had given up a career in medicine when they met Monet and Renoir at Gleyre's atelier.

Often spoken of as "the nursery of Impressionism," Gleyre's atelier became the meeting-place for four of the most important figures in the movement. There is little evidence that the four young painters immediately sympathized with each other in the cosmopolitan atmosphere of Gleyre's school, but they soon

BOUDIN
Low Tide near Honfleur
oil on wood
1854–57. 26.7 × 36.5cm
(11 × 14in)
This small-scale work is reminiscent of earlier British studies.

realized they had several interests in common one of which was landscape painting and often went on *plein-air* expeditions into the countryside around Paris. In 1921, five years before his death, Claude Monet recalled the early days:

> At Gleyre's atelier I found Renoir, Sisley, and Bazille. As we were drawing from a model . . . Gleyre criticized my work. "It's not bad," he said, "but the breast is too heavy, the shoulder too powerful, the foot too large." "I can only draw what I see," I replied timidly . . . "Praxiteles borrowed the best elements from a hundred imperfect models to create a masterpiece," retorted Gleyre drily. "One must always think of classical antiquity."

It is tempting to think that the eighty-one year old Monet's memory had perhaps grown somewhat dim (if not bitter) on the subject of Gleyre, a teacher held in the highest respect by Renoir and many other *élèves*. Nevertheless, one evening during his time at Gleyre's Monet gathered together Sisley, Renoir, and Bazille and said "*Filons d'ici!*" ("let's get out of here!") "We left," Monet said in 1921 "after two weeks . . . We were well rid of the place, because I don't think any of the most promising students in the atelier ever made good." He was wrong on both counts: his memory must indeed have been failing him, for they remained with Gleyre until he closed down in 1864; and he and his friends were the most promising students in the place!

In addition to Monet, Renoir, Bazille, and Sisley, two more young artists who were to be involved in the Impressionist movement, Paul

Cézanne and Armand Guillaumin, born in 1839 and 1841 respectively, had also gravitated to Paris by 1862. Twentieth-century art historians revere the former as the creative talent who was eventually to go beyond Impressionism, while posterity has largely forgotten the latter precisely because he became one of the most faithful exponents of the new genre.

Cézanne had come to Paris in 1861 on the urging of the novelist Emile Zola, a childhood friend from Aix-en-Provence where Cézanne's father was a banker. Cézanne had been studying law but had abandoned this to become a painter, working at the Académie Suisse. It was here that he met Armand Guillaumin, who was painting during the time off from his job for the Paris-Orléans railway, and Camille Pissarro, who introduced them both to Monet and his friends from Gleyre's atelier.

DEPICTING MODERN LIFE

1862 was certainly a year of coincidental meetings which would have great consequences for art. That year, whilst he was copying Velazquez's *Infanta Margarita* on to a copper plate at the Louvre, Edgar Degas was interrupted in his work by Edouard Manet, signalling the beginning of an extraordinary relationship between the two men. They had much in common; both were of patrician Parisian families, and neither had been greatly influenced by the *plein-air* movement. Degas and Manet were also consciously resisting Courbet's

RENOIR
Trees in the Forest
of Fontainebleau
oil on canvas
c.1860.
OPPOSITE It would be difficult to guess that this robust and literal view is by Renoir, but his interest in the effects of light, even at this early stage, is quite evident.

call for a "social realist" art. Despite the fact that circumstances link them very closely with the "true" Impressionists such as Monet and Pissarro, their own artistic concerns in painting *la vie Parisienne* were largely to hold them together and apart from the others.

Manet and Degas were great admirers of one another's work (albeit on occasion very grudgingly), but they differed greatly in matters of politics and philosophy. On the one hand, Manet was staunchly republican in his politics and a considerable intellectual who craved and enjoyed the society of writers and critics involved with the new art such as Champfleury, Duranty, Baudelaire and later Mallarmé. Degas, on the other hand, was an arch-conservative and frequently a peevish anti-intellectual.

At the Salon of 1861 Manet exhibited his *Spanish Singer* (*Le Chanteur Espagnol*) to considerable acclaim. Reminiscent of Velazquez and Goya in style and of popular interest in its Spanish subject matter, the painting nevertheless displays the beginnings of the broad brushwork and rich colouration which were to be a feature of Manet's later work. Moreover the *Spanish Singer* disdained the fine finish of the Académic style and showed a sense of Realism which challenged Courbet at his own game attracting a cabal of critics, writers, and painters – Champfleury, Baudelaire, and Henri Fantin-Latour especially – to Manet's door where he welcomed their attentions and the beginnings of fame. Much later Matisse called

Manet "the first great modern artist because his free and spontaneous brushwork liberated the artist's instincts."

In retrospect it is tempting to imagine at this time a republican-leaning, critical, artistic avant-garde armed with the desire for the untrammelled, the vigorous, the "real" in art, simply lying in wait for someone like Manet, a skillful, fresh, uncompromising and above all modern artist with metropolitan and cosmopolitan interests to come along and bear the standard of a new art. In many respects this was the case. Baudelaire, who in fact was twenty years Manet's senior, was respected as a rigorous art critic, he was a friend of Delacroix, an admirer of Courbet and lately a close friend of Manet. In 1862 Baudelaire was working on his *The Painter of Modern Life* (*Le Peintre de la vie moderne*) a critique which, as the title suggests, discusses in which direction art should go in the modern world of the big city. The subject of *The Painter of Modern Life* is not Edouard Manet, however, who was as yet relatively unknown, but Constantin Guys, an illustrator and watercolourist who had covered the Crimean War for the *Illustrated London News* and whose pictures of Parisian life brought much admiration from artists and critics alike. Baudelaire's critique concerned itself with his own time and demanded an art which could deliver it up in all its present reality, not in anachronistic Neo-Classical allegories:

The past is interesting not only because of the beauty which the

MANET
The Spanish Singer
oil on canvas
1860. 147.5 × 114.5cm
(58 × 45in)
OPPOSITE *This painting and*
The Artist's Parents *were accepted at the Salon of 1861 and received an honourable mention, a welcome distinction after the rejection of* The Absinthe Drinker *in 1859.*

MANET
Baudelaire
etching
c.1869.
ABOVE Baudelaire and Manet had met in 1858 and they were in frequent and close contact by 1860. The friendship lasted until the death of the poet in 1867. Baudelaire's views on the role of the artist in the modern world, published in 1863 as "Le Peintre de la vie moderne", were an important influence on Manet and his contemporaries.

MANET
Gypsy Woman
Smoking a Cigarette
oil on canvas
c.1862. 91 × 73cm
(36 × 29in)
OPPOSITE This is probably what the Carmen in Prosper Merrimé's original story would have looked like. However, Bizet's opera was not performed before 1875.

artists of the past – whose present it was – have extracted from it, but because of its historical value. The same applies to the present. The pleasure which we derive from the presentation of the present derives from the beauty which it may possess, as well as from its essential quality as the present. Modernity is the transitory, the fugitive, the contingent, which make up one half of art, the other being the eternal and the immutable. This transitory fugitive element, which is constantly changing, must not be despised or neglected. If you do so you tumble into the emptiness of an abstract and undefinable beauty.

Manet was shortly to prove himself to be the painter of this modern life. He was already evolving compositions with subjects such as *The Old Musician* (*Le Vieux musicien*), *The Spanish Dancers* (*Le Ballet Espagnol*) and *Lola de Valence* which, although they were not the *actualités* of Guys, represented real people. Baudelaire considered Manet to "combine a vigorous taste for reality, modern reality – already a good sign – with an imagination which is both abundant and lively . . ."

In 1859 the Salon had rejected Manet's *The Absinthe Drinker*, a painting of modern Paris in its cups, but had accepted the more innocuous *Spanish Singer* two years later. In 1862 he finished *Music in the Tuileries Gardens*, perhaps the first great painting of "modern life"; its subject matter was on one level completely up to date; the Parisian élite had recently abandoned the Palais-Royale Gardens for the

Tuileries, which was larger and closer to their residences. Whether consciously or not, Manet was answering Baudelaire's call; and whilst he was working on the subject of modern life, Degas, Monet, Sisley, Renoir, Bazille, Pissarro, Guillaumin, Cézanne, and Berthe Morisot (who later married Manet's brother, Eugène, and was a very close friend of Manet himself) were also becoming painters of the modern world. Reluctantly Manet was becoming, if not the leader of this wave of artists, then the whipping boy for the sins they were poised to commit in the art world.

Music in the Tuileries Gardens is a painting central to the development of Impressionism in that it seems to embody almost by design the transitory, the fugitive, the constantly changing. It has little in practical terms to do with the increasing desire of Monet, Pissarro, Renoir, and Sisley to find a way of capturing, in Jules Laforgue's elegant words, "nature as she is, which is to say solely by means of coloured vibrations," but it opens up a whole new realm of the possible. It is the view of a fashionable flâneur, a stroller in the park taking in the scene, a montage of frozen moments of Parisians at their leisure. We are in the age of photography after all and Manet studied photographs for some of the heads. The painting conveys movement and colour with virtuosic brushstrokes, yet the lighting is flat, the background has been scraped and smeared with the palette knife to give the impression, and not much more, of foliage; the figures at the extreme edges are real

DEGAS
Derby Day
oil on canvas c.1860–62.
26.5 × 21.5cm (10 × 9in)
BELOW This small picture is reminiscent of English sporting prints of the day.

people. Baudelaire himself is there as well as the poet Théophile Gautier, Fantin-Latour, the Inspector of Museums Baron Taylor, the sculptor and poet Zacharie Astruc, Eugène Manet and Offenbach. These people are easily discernable but the woman seated in the centre of the picture exists in a confusion of yellow and violet next to an enigmatic, two-dimensional tree.

Two paintings by Edgar Degas from this period, *The Young Spartans* and *The Gentlemen's Race: Before the Start*, both painted between 1860–1862 (and reworked in the 1880s) continued to answer the broad demands of Baudelaire, and of Edmond and Jules de Goncourt

who sought "a line which would precisely render life, embrace from close at hand the individual, the particular, a living human, inward line . . ."

The Young Spartans (*Les Jeunes Spartiates*), despite its classical theme, avoids the stock classical motifs; there are no temples or plane tree groves, the sky is not an attic blue; most importantly the figures are not characterized as Greek, but are modelled on contemporary Parisian boys and girls. The achievement is that of a thoroughly modern history painting. *The Gentlemen's Race* – together with two others, *At the Races* (*Aux Courses*) and *At the Races: The Start* (*Aux Courses: Le Départ*) – reflect the Parisian passion for the new racecourse which had opened at Longchamp in the Bois de Boulogne in 1857. The new track was a direct result of the rebuilding of Paris and presented a new venue for the *beau monde* to entertain itself; indeed some of Manet's and Degas' patrons were members of the Jockey Club which organized the races.

The new Paris being summoned into existence by Napoleon III and Haussmann was admirably suited to the realization of Baudelaire's project. The increasing wealth and number of people who made up the middle classes, the proliferation of entertainments, the sheer novelty of the new streets and squares with their airy prospects, were the new reality which a painter of modern life had to subsume in his or her

work. In retrospect, we can see that the work of Manet and Degas outdoors in the city, and that of the Gleyre students led by Monet, who were escaping Paris to paint in the nearby countryside, would eventually coincide. In his eloquent essay of 1883 Jules Laforgue formulates a definition of *plein-air* painting which declares that "the open air concept governs the entire work of Impressionist painters, and means the painting of beings and things in their appropriate atmosphere . . ." This is what, in a sense, Manet and Degas were already about as early as 1862, strolling through Paris and its environs, sketch-book in hand. In fact Degas' range of vision was much wider than that of Manet, his notebook revealing subjects which included mourners and the local undertakers.

JONGKIND
Entrance to the Port of Honfleur
oil on canvas
1864. 42 × 56cm (17 × 22in)
ABOVE Like Boudin, and later Monet, on whom he was to have a great influence, Jongkind was primarily a self-taught painter of sea and rivers based in Normandy.

MANET
Races at Longchamp
oil on canvas 1864.
44 × 85cm (17 × 34in)
OPPOSITE Longchamp was rapidly becoming an important social attraction for the wealthy bourgeois of Paris. Manet and Degas were frequent visitors.

PISSARRO
A Clearing in the Woods
oil on canvas
c.1864. 26.5 × 21cm (10 × 8in)
*OPPOSITE Although this is only a small
study, it is quite clear that the artist
had not yet found his own style.*

At this early stage in the story
of Impressionism, in a year when
Monet, Renoir, Sisley, Cézanne,
Guillaumin, Morisot, and Bazille
were still in their early twenties
and searching for something new,
the influence on them of the
plein-airistes and the Barbizon
School was still to bear substantial
fruit. Monet's links to an older
generation of landscape painters
increased when he met and
became a lasting friend of Johan
Jongkind, a Dutch artist whose

work is linked to that of Corot,
Courbet, and Monet's first real
teacher, Boudin. Meanwhile Berthe
Morisot, born the same year as
Renoir and Bazille, and daughter
of the Secretary-General of the
Crédit Financier, was working
under the encouragement of Corot.
He was teaching her landscape
painting in Fontainebleau and
Auvers where she was in frequent
contact with Daubigny whose
absolute devotion to *plein-airisme*
was uncompromising.

DAUBIGNY
The Marsh at Sunset
oil on canvas
1861. 33 × 57cm (13 × 22in)
*BELOW Daubigny, a devout plein-
airiste, had built a studio-boat to be
able to paint from the river, an example
later followed by Monet. Some critics
said that he produced nothing but
sketches and that he was satisfied
with a first impression. Others
praised his "delicious naïvety,
simple as a child, adding nothing
and removing nothing".*

MANET
Lola de Valence
oil on canvas
1862. 123 × 92cm (48 × 36in)
ABOVE Manet produced a series of Spanish pictures as the ballet company was touring Paris. He had never been to Spain at the time, and did not go there until 1865.

BAZILLE
The Pink Dress
oil on canvas
1864. 147 × 110cm (58 × 43in)
OPPOSITE This rich and finely finished piece – also known as View of a Village *– shows just how much the twenty-three-year-old artist's technique and vision were beginning to mature.*

1863: THE SALON DES REFUSÉS

. . . it is either a young man's idea of a joke, or it is a festering sore, unworthy of comment.

LOUIS ETIENNE, 1863

In 1863 the new railway line from Paris to Deauville was opened by the Duc de Morny, the internal combustion engine was invented, and in August, Eugène Delacroix, the source of so much colourful inspiration for the new artists, died. The 15th January was an ominous day for it marked the announcement by the Comte de Nieuwerkerke, the Director-General of National Museums, that the Salon (which had been held in the vast Palais de l'Industrie since the Exposition Universelle of 1855) was to be reorganized. For established artists, who had won medals at previous Salons, entry was now automatic as they did not have to pass the jury, but they were limited to three works each. The new rules were to present a serious blow to relative newcomers like Manet and Pissarro, whose work the jury was to reject later in the year.

Meanwhile Manet's first major exhibition went ahead at Louis Martinet's gallery in the boulevard des Italiens. It was here that *Music in the Tuileries Gardens* was first shown together with thirteen other paintings including *Lola de Valence* and *The Spanish Dancers*. The exhibition attracted the attention of Monet as well as Bazille who declared in a letter to his parents that one session spent looking at the Manets was worth a month of heavy work.

In April it was becoming clear that the Salon was making heavy work of its new rules. Of the 5,000 works which had been submitted, 2,783 had been rejected by the jury, led by a traditionalist of the history painting school, Emile Signol, who had once been furious with Renoir for using colour in the flamboyant style of Delacroix. In fact Delacroix and Ingres were members of the jury, but were not involved in the selection of works. All three of Manet's submissions, which included *Luncheon on the Grass* were refused entry to the exhibition.

The importance of being shown at the Salon for artists at this time cannot be underestimated. There were certainly well over a hundred independent galleries like Martinet's, but the Salon was the only marketplace with an assured audience of thousands; *le tout Paris* would be certain to be there, and failure to show at it meant another year without significant exposure to the public, the commissioning authorities, the dealers, and the critics. Although Manet had been rejected before, in 1857 and 1859, he was well aware of the benefits of appearing at the Salon and continued to strive to be accepted there as did the younger artists such as Monet and Renoir. To make things worse, several regular exhibitors had also fallen at the new

DAUMIER
The Pride of Having One's
Portrait at the Salon
lithograph 1845.
26 × 17cm (10 × 7in)
*ABOVE Honoré Daumier is best known
as a prolific and scathing caricaturist
of political and artistic events in
nineteenth-century Paris. His
paintings of contemporary life form a
less accomplished background to the
work of Manet and Degas – Manet's
teacher Thomas Couture had once
warned his pupil that he would end up
as a Daumier if he carried on in his
usual irreverent fashion.*

GÉRÔME
Christian Martyrs
oil on wood
1863–73. 88 × 150cm
(35 × 59in)
*ABOVE RIGHT Gérôme was one of the
most popular Salon artists of his
day. His taste and technique in
classical and biblical subjects was
not shared by the Impressionists.*

hurdles, artists with official com-missions already behind them who would in the normal course of events be expected to show at the Salon. One artist had even submitted works done for the Empress Eugénie – a more important patron, save the Emperor himself, could not be imagined – and had them rejected. The press seized upon the opportunity offered by the fiasco that the Salon was turning into, and the tradition-alists as well as supporters of Manet and the younger artists demanded that something should be done. In the end the Emperor paid a visit to the Salon to judge for himself and, with his wife's rejected commission no doubt firmly in his mind, he too declared that something must be done. However, the jury refused to reconvene and the exhibition had in any case already been hung. On 24th April, just three weeks before the opening of the Salon, the following announcement appeared in the *Moniteur Universel:*

> Numerous complaints have reached the Emperor on the subject of works of art which have

been refused by the jury of the Exhibition. His Majesty, wishing to allow the public to judge the legitimacy of these complaints, has decided that the rejected works shall be exhibited in another part of the Palais de l'Industrie. This exhibition will be voluntary, and artists who do not wish to participate need only to inform the administration of the exhibition, which will hasten to return their works to them.

In a sense Napoleon III had pulled off another coup; this time he had succeeded in showing himself as an enlightened liberal ruler concerned with art and ready to listen to public opinion. The press enjoyed a field day on this issue not least because there were few other caus-es for them to champion under the strict regime of censorship that had then been imposed by the Emperor.

The new exhibition came to be known as the Salon des Refusés, and, when it opened its doors directly adjacent to the Salon proper on 17th May, over 10,000 people came to marvel at it. Amongst the jumble of paintings which had been hung with no particular order or care (of course

MEISSONIER
French Campaign, Napoleon
oil on canvas
1864. 49 × 75cm (19 × 30in)
BELOW Edifying subjects, whether religious or heroic or both, were the staple diet of the Salon during the second half of the century.

CABANEL
Birth of Venus
oil on canvas
1863. 130 × 225cm
(51 × 89in)
ABOVE LEFT The star of the official 1863 Salon, Cabanel's Venus *embodies perfectly all that Manet, Degas and the nascent Impressionists were trying to avoid. The highly finished, quintessentially classical composition with its hint of eroticism was bought by Napoleon III. On show next door in the Salon des Refusés, Manet's frankly realist* Luncheon on the Grass *drew outrage and condemnation.*

many pictures which deserved to be rejected were on show) were two which caused an especially violent reaction, James McNeill Whistler's *White Girl* which had previously been rejected by the Royal Academy in London, and Manet's *Luncheon on the Grass*. Whistler's painting was ridiculed by many whilst "Manet in the furthest hall," as the *refusé* Jean-Charles Cazin observed, "went right through the wall with his *Luncheon on the Grass*." If *Music in the Tuileries Gardens* had caused a positive stir amongst his fellow artists and the Spanish paintings had delighted the public, *Luncheon on the Grass* was an instant succès de scandale.

Manet's technique aside, the general public was outraged at the depiction of a female nude together with two clothed young bourgeois, and Napoleon III pronounced it to be an offence against modesty. (The Emperor was not too modest however to purchase Alexandre Cabanel's studiously academic but erotic *Birth of Venus* (*La Naissance de Vénus*), which was on show in the official Salon next door to the *refusés*.) Zola defended the picture

by drawing attention to the fact that there were several paintings in the Louvre with clothed and nude figures. Zacharie Astruc also leapt to Manet's defence, going so far as to publish a newspaper *Le Salon de 1863* which called Manet "one of the greatest artistic characters of the time," lauding his work for "brilliance, inspiration, power, flavour, surprise." Manet professed himself to be distressed by all this attention, complaining to his friend Baudelaire that abuse was raining down on him like hail.

Manet's painting had ultimately derived from a work of 1510–11 in the Louvre (by Titian, Giorgione, or both) known as *La Fête champêtre*; it also had a respectable precedent in an engraving by Marcantonio after Raphael. Yet the flat yellowish lighting on the central nude depicts her without a trace of the customary *pudeur* so obvious and conventionally appealing in Cabanel's pinkly suffused Venus, the star of the "official" Salon. One critic, Théophile Burger, a friend of Baudelaire's "[failed] to see what could have induced a distinguished and intelligent artist to adopt such an absurd composition." But he admitted that "there are qualities of colour and light in the landscape, and indeed some very fine passages of modelling in the torso." These fine passages were passed over in a pamphlet by Louis Etienne who pronounced what was on everyone's mind, describing the painting as:

> A nonchalant *bréda* [a prostitute] ... completely naked, impudently lounges between two dandies dressed up to the nines. They give the impression of two students on holiday who are behaving outrageously, to try and give the impression of real men . . . It is either a young man's idea of a joke, or it is a festering sore, unworthy of comment.

The prostitute in Manet's painting is referred to by Etienne as a *bréda* after the rue Bréda in the Batignolles district of Paris where the women worked. At the time of the Salon des Refusés Manet lived and worked nearby. It was in the Café Guerbois at 11 Grande rue des Batignolles that a group of like-minded artists and intellectuals, amongst them Manet, Monet, Pissarro, Bazille, Degas, Renoir, Zola, and Nadar would meet in the coming years to discuss their life and work. They became known as the Batignolles Group.

Zola's view, fortunately the one that has prevailed, was that:

> What you have to look for in the picture is not just the picnic on the grass, but the whole landscape with its bold and subtle passages, its broadly painted, solid foreground, its light and delicate background and that firm flesh modelled in broad areas of light, those supple and strong pigments, and,

particularly, that delicate splash of white among the green leaves in the background; in fact to look at the whole of this vast, airy composition, at this attention to nature, rendered with such accurate simplicity.

Festering sore or airy composition, *Luncheon on the Grass* pushed modern life into the Salon and out into the world even though it was literally and figuratively one of the *peintures refusées*. Nowadays we find it extremely difficult to find anything scandalous in this picture, but at the time nudes were only acceptable in certain highly stylized and sanitized forms like Cabanel's. The "real thing" was wholly intolerable.

One more event was to cause uproar that year. In a decree dated 13th November the government announced sweeping reforms of the Ecole des Beaux-Arts, removing it from the control of the Académie des Beaux-Arts, installing a system of ateliers to teach painting within the Ecole which had previously only taught drawing, and abolishing several important competitions, one of which was the Prix de Paysage Historique. Many of the Barbizon

MANET
Luncheon on the Grass
oil on canvas 1863.
208 × 264.5cm (82 × 104in)
Neither the critics nor public could accept a classical scene in modern dress, and although there were several precedents for this subject in the Louvre, the shock of seeing a female nude in the company of two modern-day dandies was simply too much. The flat lighting and uncompromising realism in the depiction of the main figures also brought much criticism of Manet's technique.

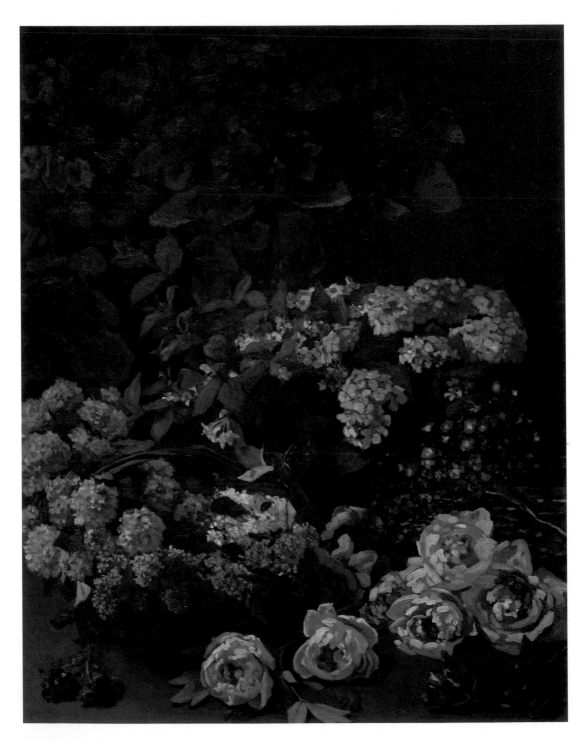

landscapists had taken part in the competition; Rousseau and Daubigny had both attempted it and, as art historian Albert Boime points out, Corot and Gleyre had trained their students to compete for it whilst Monet and Sisley were both interested in it. The government had decreed the reforms partly under the pretext that they would foster more originality, but they were popular with neither the Académie nor the students, who feared they would no longer be able to choose which master they worked under in preparation for the Ecole. Sisley was one of those who signed a petition protesting against the changes, proving, according to Albert Boime, that the group of students of Gleyre's atelier had not yet relinquished hope of official recognition through the Ecole's competition structure and the official Salon to which they still aspired, despite the success of the Salon des Refusés.

1864–1866: "OLYMPIA WAKES"

In 1864 the Duc de Morny, who organized the building of a coastal resort at Deauville and connected it to Paris with a railway line so that affluent Parisians could take advantage of it, inaugurated the new race track there. Nothing was unusual about this commonplace development in an era of rapid industrial and economic expansion in France. It is simply another example of the new middle-class prosperity and (expensive) free time which many could now spend in a variety of pursuits. That year the

first international victory at Longchamp by a French racehorse was celebrated. Speed was of the moment; the railway had already revolutionized travel and was helping France on its way to becoming a major industrial power.

The Second Empire was attempting to extend its power base in other ways too; in Mexico Napoleon III installed Maximilian of Austria as the puppet ruler, but like so much of the Emperor's foreign policy, this was to prove a disastrous chimera. Meanwhile,

FANTIN-LATOUR
Flowers and Fruit
oil on canvas
1865. 64 × 57cm (25 × 22in)
ABOVE Fantin-Latour's paintings of flowers sold particularly well in London where he was seen as the highly desirable face of French art.

MONET
Spring Flowers
oil on canvas
1864. 117 × 89cm (46 × 35in)
OPPOSITE This early piece proves that Monet was able to produce commercially accessible work.

Eugène Chevreul published his second work on colour, and Charles Gleyre was forced to close down his atelier due to failing health and lack of funds. In the summer Morisot, Renoir, and Pissarro had work accepted at the Salon which was now to be run annually. Manet, however, was rejected and out of the limelight for a year.

With the demise of Gleyre's atelier, Monet and his friends took off to the country to paint. In the early spring Monet had been working in and around Fontainebleau with Renoir and Sisley. That summer Monet returned to the Normandy coast at a farm near Honfleur, where Bazille, Boudin, and Jongkind later joined him. Bazille had returned to Paris when Monet wrote to him from Honfleur, entreating him to come back to the country and declaring that:

> It really is appallingly difficult to do something which is complete in every way, and I think most people are content with mere approximations . . . I intend to battle on, scrape off, and start again . . . and when I look at nature I feel as if I'll be able to paint it all, note it all down . . . it's on the strength of observation and reflection that one finds a way. So we must dig and delve unceasingly.

FANTIN-LATOUR
Tannhäuser on the Venusberg
oil on canvas
1864. 98 × 130cm
(39 × 51in)
Fantin-Latour had discovered Wagner the previous year. Tannhäuser *failed in Paris but Fantin-Latour adored the music of Wagner and Berlioz, an enthusiasm shared by Bazille.*

MANET
Christ Mocked by the Soldiers
oil on canvas 1865.
191.5 × 148.5cm (75 × 59in)
ABOVE "You are the foremost in the decrepitude of your art", Baudelaire wrote in a vitriolic vein to an extremely unhappy Manet after the scandal of Olympia *and* Christ Mocked *had broken at the Salon. Both paintings were taken down from their prominent position and rehung in the darkest corner of Room M.*

CARAVAGGIO
Ecce Homo
oil on canvas 1606.
128 × 103cm (50 × 41in)
ABOVE RIGHT Caravaggio's naturalism was considered outrageous at a time when most subjects were idealized and sanitized; Manet suffered the same fate.

The influence of Boudin and especially Jongkind is clearly evident in Monet's work from this early period. He even admitted to touches of Corot in some of the landscapes he was producing near Honfleur. But *Rue de la Barolle* and *Farmyard in Normandy* (*La Ferme Normande*), both painted at this time, display the beginnings of his rapidly developing technique. At this point he was producing work at a phenomenal rate and he continued to do so for the rest of his life; his head was, as he wrote to Bazille in July 1864, "bursting with the desire to paint." This was just as well, for he lived on the edge of destitution and often had to call on friends like Bazille to help him out of financial difficulties. His diligence paid off in the next year's Salon where two works were accepted, along with Degas' first successful submission and what proved to be his last history painting, *Scene of War in the Middle Ages* (*Scène de guerre au Moyen Age*).

Monet showed two seascapes at the Salon of 1865, *The Mouth of the Seine at Honfleur* (*L'Embouchure de la*

Seine à Honfleur) and *Pointe de la Hève at Low Tide* (*Pointe de la Hève à marée basse*). In both the influence of Jongkind and Boudin is evident, but the critic Gallet was moved to describe Monet as "a young realist who promises much. His two seascapes . . . display the work of a powerful hand uninterested in prettiness and greatly preoccupied with accuracy of effect." Another critic, Victor Fournel, offered a withering dismissal: "What is there to say, for instance, about this *Mouth of the Seine at Honfleur*? The waves are represented by lumps of earth, the sails of the boats by triangles of black wood: one might well think it had been scrawled by a child of twelve on the cover of his Sunday school book." But both Monet and Degas, as well as Pissarro, who was again successful at the Salon, were

to be overshadowed by Edouard Manet and his *Olympia*.

Earlier in 1865 Manet had again exhibited at the Galerie Martinet to some acclaim. In May the Salon opened to a hysterical onslaught. The objects of the critics' scorn and the public's distaste were Manet's two submissions, *Christ Mocked by the Soldiers* (*Jésus insulté par les soldats*) and *Olympia*. Hanging together, they attracted crowds of curious viewers. The critic Victor de Jankovitz waxed sardonic: "Thanks to his brushwork, *Christ Mocked* by M. Manet, is a picture beneath all criticism. It is Raphael as corrected by a third-rate Courbet." *Christ Mocked by the Soldiers* came away from its confrontation with the critics fairly unscathed in comparison with *Olympia*. Gentlewomen were said

INGRES
Sleeping Odalisque
oil on canvas
1829. 30 × 47.5cm (12 × 19in)
It might be that Ingres' nude is more provocative and erotic than Olympia, *but nevertheless she is devoid of the plain everyday look of Manet's model, too easily linked to prostitution by a hypocritical bourgeois society.*

to have averted their eyes from the shameful sight. Nevertheless they and their gentlemen-folk crushed into Room M to assure themselves of the veracity of the shocking reports.

Olympia's notoriety quickly transcended that of *Luncheon on the Grass* which, it should be remembered, had been shown outside the official Salon as a work which had been rejected as being unworthy of recognition. The Salon catalogue entry for the painting carried the following verse by the painter's friend Zacharie Astruc:

When, weary of dreaming,
Olympia wakes,
Springtime arrives in the arms of a
gentle black envoy;
It is the slave, like unto a night
of passion,
Who comes to make the day bloom,
a delight to behold;
The august young girl in whom
the flame burns.

Everything about the painting – the disposition of its subject, her dishevelled sheets and her scant accoutrements, the black maid, the little black cat, the flowers, the technique, with some passages finely modelled and some blocked in with broad sweeps of the brush – conspired to confuse and dismay its viewers. There was little doubt that this was another *bréda*, a prostitute, weary, not from dreaming, but from a night of work. Paris was awash with prostitutes; from the poorest streetwalker in the rue Bréda to the richest *courtesane*, lavishly

TITLE

TITIAN
The Venus of Urbino
oil on canvas
c.1538. 120 × 165cm
(47 × 65in)
An archetype for Olympia.
The compositional similarities between this and Manet's painting are obvious.

entertaining in apartments along the *grands boulevards*. But painting them, other than in the enciphered form of a Venus or some demi-goddess, was unheard of until the first Salon des Refusés and now *Olympia*. Manet had liberated a new territory which others, Degas in particular, were later able to exploit with more or less impunity. Directly based on a pose much used by sixteenth-century Italian painters, the English painter Peter Lely, and eighteenth-century French artists such as François Boucher, *Olympia* did not try to charm the public. Here was a real woman, unashamed, addressing the viewer directly and without pretence or any attempt at seduction.

The Second Empire was all artifice. Away from the massive façades of the new Paris designed by Haussmann, half of the population, which Haussmann himself had described as "living in poverty bordering on destitution," was in the process of being relocated to featureless *faubourgs* (suburbs) or concentrated into areas like Belleville. It is significant that one critic openly described Olympia as *une petite faubourienne*, which is to say a common working-class girl, not as *une cocotte*, the euphemism most commonly used. The hypocrisy of the time may appear to be staggering, but it was a hypocrisy which tolerated its *courtesanes* as long as they hovered above the dirt and grime of reality. Manet broke the silence in this respect so thoroughly that, as T.J. Clark has penetratingly observed, it caused a

MANET
Olympia
oil on canvas
1863. 130.5 × 190cm (51 × 75in)
This painting caused a storm verging on outrage at the Salon of 1865, and established Manet's reputation and fame, though not, perhaps, in the way he had immediately hoped. It has been referred to as a turning point in the history of modern art, combining with Luncheon on the Grass *to entirely subvert the traditional artistic view of the nude, as it was previously encapsulated in the Titian painting* The Venus of Urbino, *an archetype for* Olympia.

MONET
Luncheon on the Grass
oil on canvas 1865–66.
130 × 181cm
(51 × 71in)
A sketch of the unfinished work.

crisis in the language of art criticism itself. Far from being lost for words, the arbiters of the nation's taste, from the meanest hack to the loftiest intellectual, were volubly falling over each other to avoid describing *Olympia* in traditional terms. Whilst they were busy likening Olympia's skin to India rubber, all but two of them could not or would not see the obvious reference to Titian's *Venus of Urbino* which Manet had once copied in oil at the Uffizi in Florence. The irony of calling a *faubourienne* "Olympia" was not however lost on them; any one of the several licensed brothels in Paris would have offered up a number of women working under the classical *noms de guerre* of Olympia, Lucretia, Calliope or the most popular, Virginia. The chief problem for the critics and public alike was that *Olympia* had appeared *dans le Salon-même*, and this had stretched their tolerance beyond reason and their reason beyond tolerance. The outcry against the painting and its companion *Christ Mocked* was so great that they were eventually both removed to the furthest, darkest corner of the huge Palais de l'Industrie. Manet's fame (or infamy) was assured for the rest of his life. His position as the reluctant champion of the new artists of modern life was affirmed once and for all.

In the world at large life and death went on: across the Atlantic Ocean in the United States President Abraham Lincoln was assassinated, in Paris the First Communist International was held, and in England a young

mathematics don at Christ Church College, Oxford, published a story called *Alice in Wonderland* under the pseudonym of Lewis Carroll.

Encouraged by his own reception at the Salon, albeit mixed, and the example of Manet, Claude Monet had embarked in 1865 on his own monumental *Luncheon on the Grass*, obviously intended to make a much bigger splash in the Paris art world. Sadly the painting was abandoned in March 1866, when the deadline for that year's Salon expired, and survives only in

MONET
Women in the Garden
oil on canvas
1865–66. 418 × 150cm
(165 × 59in)
This is Monet's last attempt at a large-scale figure composition. Two possible sources for the picture's inspiration are thought to have been a photograph of his friend Bazille's sisters and a costume illustration from a fashion magazine. Camille posed for no fewer than three of the figures.

DEGAS
Woman with Chrysanthemums
oil on canvas
1865. 71 × 92cm
(28 × 36in)
*Although he used a photograph
to make this picture, Degas also
made exhaustive preliminary
studies from life.*

fragments and an oil sketch of what was once a vast picture almost fifteen feet high by twenty feet wide. Monet left the canvas in Bazille's studio for years as security against unpaid rent before he reclaimed it, by which time part of it had gone mouldy. Monet removed this portion and cut the remainder into two sections. The sketch for the painting indicates that Monet's conception was for a major *plein-air* work, using the relatively novel idea of figures sketched on the spot; these included Sisley, Bazille, and Monet's mistress, Camille Doncieux. By all accounts Monet was obsessed with the massive project and spent the whole of the summer of 1865, as the *Olympia* scandal raged in Paris, devoted to it. He frequently begged Bazille by post to come down to the forest of Fontainebleau and sit for him. Throughout his work on the painting Monet was harrassed: firstly he was hampered by an injury to his leg in 1865 and then, having moved to Bazille's Paris studio in order to finish the picture for the 1866 Salon, he was forced to leave the studio and move across the river to another. Unable to complete the painting, Monet furiously produced (in four days) a full-length portrait of Camille known as *The Woman in the Green Dress* (*Femme en vert*), which in turn proved a success at the Salon.

Luncheon on the Grass was a prodigious undertaking in every respect; and as Andrew Forge has suggested, "It was something as different from Courbet's earthy social analysis as it was from Manet's sophisticated reflections on the

erotic in modern life. Monet was trying to present on an exhibition scale that particular area of painting that was specific to the direct study. He was trying to monumentalize the syntax of a sketch."

Undaunted by his failure to complete *Luncheon on the Grass*, in early 1866 Monet embarked on another large picture, nine feet by six feet in size, the *Women in the Garden* (*Femmes dans un jardin*). He had rented a house near Paris and dug a trench for the painting to be lowered into by pulleys so that he could work without moving his position relative to the subjects in front of him. The idea, ridiculed by Courbet, was to complete the whole picture *en plein air*. The painting was finished but the Salon of 1867 rejected it, a bitter blow to Monet.

THE BATIGNOLLES GROUP

The year 1866 saw the invention of dynamite by Alfred Nobel. In France Napoleon III ordered the withdrawal of his forces from Mexico, a move that was to have disastrous consequences for the puppet Emperor Maximilian. In his own salvo of explosive prose, Zola published an article entitled "Mon Salon en L'Evénement" defending the work of Cézanne, Bazille, Monet, and Pissarro and supporting a letter Cézanne had written to the Comte de Nieuwerkerke demanding another Salon des Refusés. In it Cézanne had felt obliged to "content myself with pointing out to you again that I cannot accept the unlawful judgement of colleagues to whom I have not personally given the task of assessing me . . . I wish to make a direct appeal to the public and have my work exhibited without any restriction."

A complex network of relationships between Monet, Pissarro, Bazille, Cézanne, Guillaumin, Morisot, Renoir, Sisley, Manet, and Degas had already begun to form by this point. During the private view of the 1866 Salon Monet and Bazille had encountered Manet and his entourage leaving the exhibition. Monet's signature on his *Woman in the Green Dress* had been mistaken for Manet's, who had entered the Salon to a chorus of acclaim for his supposed work. Monet recounted the story in 1900 to *Le Temps*:

> . . . imagine his consternation when he discovered that the picture about which he was being congratulated was actually by me! The saddest part of all was that on leaving the Salon he came across a group which included Bazille and me. "How goes it?" one of them asked. "Awful," replied Manet, "I am digusted. I have been complimented on a painting which is not mine."

PISSARRO
The Railway Bridge at Pontoise
oil on canvas
c.1865. 50 × 65cm
(20 × 26in)
Pissarro and his family moved to live in Pontoise, a village on the river Oise (seen here) near Auvers, in 1867, about two years after this picture was painted.

RENOIR
The Park of St Cloud
oil on canvas
1866. 50 × 61cm
(20 × 24in)
An early, surprisingly
impressionistic painting
by Renoir painted three
years before the work with
Monet at La Grenouillère.

The next day Manet is supposed to have refused to be introduced to Monet because he was still bitter about Monet's purely unintentional slight on the young master. But as Monet recalled:

> It was only in 1869 that I saw him again, and then we at once became firm friends. At our first meeting he invited me to join him every evening at a café in the Batignolles district where he and his friends gathered at the end of the day to talk. There I met Fantin-Latour, Cézanne, Degas . . . the art critic Duranty, Emile Zola and many others. For my part I used to take Sisley, Bazille, and Renoir there. Nothing could have been more interesting than the discussions we had, with their perpetual clash of opinions. They kept our wits sharpened, encouraged us to press ahead with our own experiments, and provided us with the enthusiasm to keep on painting for weeks on end until our ideas became clear and coherent . . . we emerged more finely tempered, our resolve firmer, our thoughts clearer and less confused.

1866 marks the beginnings of what came to be known as the Batignolles Group. Whilst Monet, Bazille, Renoir, Sisley, and Pissarro were working in the country, the Batignolles area of Paris was becoming a focus of artistic attention. During Haussmannization this area of Paris had expanded greatly, along with the large new boulevard des Batignolles. Between 1842 and 1866 the population of the district had increased from 15,000 to 200,000. Its position away from the centre of the city but close to the Gare St Lazare made it popular. The buildings were modern, comfortably bourgeois, and the area had become residential but still affordable. A letter of Renoir's to his parents a couple of years later when he and Bazille lived in the rue de la Paix confirms this, "Tell Mama not to worry, the Batignolles is a quiet area and cheaper than the rest of Paris."

Parts of the old village of Batignolles remained, populated by poor immigrants, rag-pickers, and prostitutes, amongst whom Manet found some of his subjects and models. Manet had lived there for some time at various addresses and had recently begun to haunt the Café Guerbois at 11 rue des Batignolles. During the next three years practically everyone of importance to Impressionism began to gather there in the evenings – Thursday nights were the favourite – to talk about art and literature. If Gleyre's atelier had been the nursery of the *plein-air* Impressionists, the Café Guerbois was undoubtedly its common room. Anyone looking for the artistic avant-garde in Paris would need go no further than the Café Guerbois, one of many cafés that had sprung up in the new Paris of wide pavements and rolling boulevards. Manet was certainly the first amongst his peers and held court with aplomb. The writer and critic of Impressionism Armand Silvestre described Manet as a revolutionary with the manners of a perfect gentleman: "he had in the extraordinary vivacity of his gaze and the mocking expression on his lips a very strong dose of the Parisian street urchin. He had a marvellous command of the annihilating and devastating phrase." Yet he still yearned for official recognition.

1867–1868: LA VILLE LUMIÈRE

The year 1867 brought with it crisis for the Second Empire. Since the proclamation of Napoleon III as Emperor in 1852 France had spent itself into a prosperity that was in essence conservative and favoured the middle and upper classes. The new boulevards and buildings of Paris were symbolic of this prosperity, as were the resorts springing up on the Normandy coast. But they had all been constructed on credit and the equivalent of the modern junk bond. In 1866 the Crédit Mobilier, which had financed a great part of the new Empire, found itself with a monumental liquidity problem. Its shares fell the next year from 1,982 francs to just 140 francs. The Mexican fiasco ended with the death of Maximilian who was abandoned by the French and

GOYA
The Third of May
oil on canvas
1814. 266 × 345cm
(105 × 136in)

MONET
The Garden of the Princess
oil on canvas
1867. 92 × 62cm (36 × 24in)
*This was one of three works that the
Louvre allowed Monet to paint on its
balcony. It shows the influence of
photography in the angle of the
view and the seemingly arbitrary
points at which the subject is cut
off by its framing.*

executed by rebels. Manet, who rightly saw this crisis as a failure of imperial politics, began a painting of the execution, making use of photographs, but also basing part of its composition on Goya's *The Third of May* which he had seen in Madrid in 1865. He was given to understand by the Salon that it would not be admitted on the grounds of its political sensitivity. A lithograph of the picture was officially banned by the censors.

Elsewhere in the world tensions ran high. In an attempt to help the Papal States French battalions were dispatched to Rome to defend them against the revolutionary Garibaldi. As usual relations with Prussia were tense. In January Napoleon III had announced constitutional changes with a move towards representative government for the Empire, but it was to be of no avail. The American Civil War had disrupted cotton trade, and the vineyards were suffering from the phylloxera disease which had appeared in 1863 and taken hold, steadily reducing the crop. The outward success of the Second Empire had, as Alastair Horne claims, "blinded French eyes to the realities beneath the surface. Syphilis was rampant and many of the great Frenchmen of the age were to die of it; Maupassant, Jules Goncourt, Dumas *fils*, Baudelaire [in 1867], and Manet. The dread disease was symptomatic of the Second Empire itself; on the surface, all gaiety and light; below, sombre purulence, decay, and ultimately death."

A visitor to Paris in the summer of 1867, and there were thousands,

would have been hard pressed to believe all this doom, for the second Exposition Universelle had taken over a city which was already crammed with hundreds of theatres and cafés, all full of Parisians enjoying themselves. Visitors to the Prussian display of armaments marvelled at the Krupp artillery pieces. The implements of modern warfare certainly looked impressive and if the French had taken more stock of them they might have thought twice about engaging the Prussians in battle a couple of years later. A picture by Manet painted at the time, *View of the Paris World's Fair* (*Vue de Paris pendant l'Exposition Universelle*) shows the French and English lighthouses erected for the Fair and the photographer Nadar's balloon, known as "The Giant", hovering over the city. Renoir's *Champs-Elysées during the Paris Fair of 1867* (*Les Champs-Elysées pendant l'Exposition Universelle de 1867*) depicts leisurely strollers; the women wear summer dresses, the sky is temptingly blue with fluffy clouds. In the background a *tricolor* flies over the Palais de l'Industrie which had been built for the previous Exposition Universelle when Pissarro had marvelled at the Corots and when Courbet's Realist Pavilion had challenged the establishment.

The same was to occur in 1867. Again Courbet erected a pavilion to rival the official Salon, and Manet, who had boycotted the Salon in disgust at having been rejected again, did the same. Pressure for another Salon des Refusés was strong: Monet, Renoir, Pissarro, Sisley, Jongkind, Manet, and

Daubigny had all signed a petition to the authorities requesting one, but the *refusés* request was rejected. Unfortunately, Manet's pavilion did scant business. Times were getting harder for the avant-garde painters. The arbitrariness of the Salon juries who changed their views on what was acceptable from year to year was a cause of intense frustration. In May Bazille had written to his parents outlining a plan which had emerged among the group to:

> . . . rent a big studio every year where we will be able to show as many of our paintings as we want. We will invite the painters we like to send paintings. Courbet, Corot, Diaz, Daubigny and many others with whom you may not be familiar have promised to send their work and strongly approve of the idea. With the latter, and Monet who is better than all of us, we are sure to succeed.

The plan came to nothing; the funds to mount the exhibition could not be found amongst the contributors, but this was essentially the first attempt to launch the *Société anonyme des artistes peintres, sculpteurs, graveurs, etc*, which upstaged the Salon of 1874.

In the meantime Claude Monet had gained permission from the

MONET
Beach at Sainte-Adresse
oil on canvas
c.1867. 75 × 101cm (30 × 40in)
Monet never tired of painting the coast of Normandy in his youth, and he worked along this stretch of coastline nearly all his life.

RENOIR
Rose Field
oil on canvas
Undated. 33 × 46.5cm
(13 × 18in)
Renoir's loose style was at the vanguard of Impressionism, but the artist later found that it was too limiting.

Louvre to paint from one of its second floor balconies. One of the three pictures that resulted is the *Garden of the Princess* (*Le Jardin de la princesse*). This, and the views of the *Quai du Louvre*, and *Saint-Germain l'Auxerrois* mark what Forge has called "crucial experiments in which [Monet] seems to be pushing the principles of Realism to their furthest limits." The *Garden of the Princess* indicates a new vision of the city using the technique Monet had been developing in his landscapes and the two large-scale figure paintings. The angle of the view shows the influence of the framing and distortive effects of photography which tend to "wrap"

the field of vision at the edges and cut off the composition at arbitrary points producing a vertiginous sense of height, distance, and space. Monet's landscapist's eye, however, shows the crowds down below as a mobile element of the cityscape rendered with the swift brush-strokes later to be denounced as "tongue-lickings". The much altered topography of Paris attracted many of Monet's friends. They could also hope to sell paintings of the new Haussmann boulevards which were not controversial subjects.

Visitors to the Exposition Universelle were seduced and intrigued that year by the exhibition of Japanese prints and artefacts which soon launched an enduring fashion for all things Japanese. Many artists were influenced by the composition of these prints, especially Degas, like Whistler before him. Japanese prints had trickled in to Europe from the 1850s, mainly used to wrap artefacts. Following several centuries of seclusion, at last Japan opened its doors to the West in 1867, and two shops in Paris were selling this new exotica. The studios of Whistler, Manet, Degas, and Monet were graced with Japanese china, fans, and prints, and these feature in several later paintings. Castagnary even called the Batignolles Group "the Japanese of painting". Monet said, that "[the Japanese] refinement of taste has always pleased me, and I approve of their aesthetic doctrine which evokes the presence of something by a shadow; and the whole by means of a fragment." Degas' work was increasingly reinforced by the Japanese print masters' sense of space and (to Western eyes) unusual perspectives and framings, as well as their subject matter which was often urban and refined. This new view was much in keeping with Degas' artistic interests.

Napoleon III's last years in power were marked by an increasing desire on his part to free up the country's moribund political and social system. Accordingly, in 1868 new laws allowed limited freedom of the press and the right to assembly for the first time since the First Republic. In a move symptomatic of the decline of the Second Empire, Baron Haussmann

was forced to approach the ruling Legislative Body and request a loan to pay for the rebuilding of Paris which amounted to a quarter of the whole French budget. Haussmann was almost finished, but so was Paris.

Manet, Degas, Morisot, Pissarro, Monet, Sisley, and Bazille all made it into the Salon of 1868 after the dismal failure of the previous year and they had François Daubigny to thank because he had been invited to sit on the jury. Daubigny's inclusion was a sign that *plein-airisme* had finally been accepted by the Salon as a legitimate method of painting, although this did not make it any easier for the avant-garde. To artists like Manet, Bazille, and Degas, who

DEGAS
Orchestra of the Paris Opera
oil on canvas
1868–69. 56.5 × 46cm
(22 × 18in)
A fine example of the new theory of composition that the Impressionists were beginning to shape. The figures are caught as though in a photograph – cut off at seemingly random points, and standing at odd angles to the artist. This is very different from the highly stylized, carefully posed and fully framed tableaux of the classical schools, and represented a radical departure.

MANET
The Balcony
oil on canvas
1868–69. 170 × 124cm
(67 × 49in)
Berthe Morisot had met Manet two
months before she posed for this
painting. Their friendship lasted
until his death in 1883.

were reasonably wealthy, not selling their work did not ultimately mean starvation.

Monet himself had none of the luxuries of a Manet or a Bazille; he was forced to sell or starve, and since he had few buyers in the late 1860s the latter fate stared him and his wife relentlessly in the face. In 1867 he had been forced by his family (on whom he relied for an allowance) to abandon Camille, then pregnant with a son, Jean. In June 1868 Monet had to ask Bazille (once again) to help him out by sending Camille some money to support herself and the child. In his begging letter he signs himself, "Your loyal and tormented friend," and adds curtly and ominously, "I was so upset yesterday that I was foolish enough to throw myself into the water. Fortunately no harm was done." It seems that Monet was too much in love with painting and life to make a serious attempt at suicide even though his despair was deep.

Despite the collapse of the Crédit Foncier and Haussmann's exorbitant claims on the national budget, *la ville lumière* thrived. Paris in the early part of 1868 was depicted with increasing acuity and originality by artists. Degas, the most consistent of the "slice of life" painters, spent all of his time in the streets, cafés, theatres, and concert halls of the city; noting, sketching, and observing with a sharp eye the effervescent activity around him. Not a *plein-airiste* by any stretch of the imagination, he composed his pictures very carefully *post hoc* in the studio. His *Orchestra of the Paris Opera* (*L'Orchestre de l'Opéra de Paris*) of 1868–69 is an excellent example of both his devotion to Ingres, his finely detailed technique and a thoroughly modern sense of composition: again the influence of photography is evident, with the figures cropped by the edges of the painting and the double-bassist turning his back to us looking at a conductor "out of shot". One of the second violinists is even captured gazing up at the incandescent tutus of the ballerinas, obviously bored with his part.

Away from the bustle of the city, Bazille was succeeding to a great extent in meshing the forms of landscape and figure painting which had been started and abandoned by Monet. *View of the Village* (*Paysage avec un village*) and *The Family Reunion* (*La Réunion de Famille*) show the influence of Manet and Monet, but taking a firm grip on the elements of the pictures. Bazille is especially fearless in the use of bright colours applied in flat areas. Berthe Morisot said of the *View of the Village*, "He is seeking what we have all so often sought: how to place a figure in outdoor surroundings. This time I think he has succeeded."

Whilst Monet, Renoir, Bazille, and Sisley had been working in and around Paris and on the coast, Camille Pissarro (older than them by ten years and yet stylistically much more a part of their generation than Manet or Degas) had been living in Pontoise, a town to the northwest of Paris where in 1866 he had settled with his mistress, Julie Vellay. His frequent visits to Paris included the Café Guerbois where he expressed himself openly and eloquently in matters of art and politics: he was a radical republican, an anarchist in fact. Thanks to Daubigny two of Pissarro's views of the *Hermitage at Pontoise* (*L'Ermitage à Pontoise*) were shown at the Salons of 1868 and 1869. They were attacked as being vulgar, coarse, primitive daubings. The paint is certainly applied with vigour and Pissarro's denial of detail and his concentration on structure using planes of colour prefigures the later work of Cézanne. But

Zola considered that "the originality here is deeply human, not derived from a mere facility of hand or a falsification of nature: it stems from the temperament of the painter himself and comprises a feeling for truth resulting from an inner conviction."

1869: "ROTTEN SKETCHES"

The French elections of May 1869 produced a massive upsurge of support for the opposition parties – mostly varying shades of republicanism. Government control of the Legislative Body was sharply reduced and the Prime Minister was forced to resign. Haussmann's fortunes continued to wane as his opponents questioned the exorbitantly high cost of his rebuilding of Paris. Napoleon III's "Liberal Empire" was in its last days. A left-wing slogan frequently heard on the streets of the big cities was "Moderation is Death".

The convulsive politics of the Empire must have been on the agenda at the Café Guerbois, but of more prurient interest may well have been the erroneous gossip amorously linking Manet and Berthe Morisot who had been introduced to the clique via Fantin-Latour. At this stage gentlewomen were not in the habit of frequenting gentlemen's café societies, so Morisot's acquaintance with Manet would have been consolidated outside the auspices of the Café Guerbois, and thus she would have been denied what Monet had called the "constant clash of opinions" and the lapidary wit-sharpening of Thursday nights.

MANET
Study for The Balcony
pencil and wash on paper
1868.
Manet was a diligent technician, and spent endless days in the Louvre copying the works of the great masters when he was a student at Couture's atelier. His wish to evolve from the masters, rather than to reject them, is reflected here in his use of the classical methodology of producing a careful study for a larger work.

she had posed a few months after they had met at the Louvre, where she was also a copyist. Manet's ponderous influence on Berthe can be seen in a portrait of her sister, Edma, and her mother which Manet had retouched into what Berthe called "the prettiest little caricature". For her part Berthe, who had been brought up by Corot and Daubigny as a *plein-airiste*, encouraged Manet to take to the outdoors and lighten his otherwise sombre palette. At this time another woman painter, Eva Gonzalès, the daughter of a novelist, appeared on Manet's horizon and much to Berthe Morisot's dismay he agreed to take Eva as his pupil – the first and last time he chose to teach.

In the spring of 1869 Monet had installed himself in the village of Saint-Michel near Bougival. This was an increasingly popular resort on the Seine linked to Paris by the Paris–Saint-Germain railway and the stop at Chatou. This area had

RENOIR
La Grenouillère
oil on canvas
1869. 66 × 86cm
(26 × 34in)
ABOVE Renoir and Monet painted a series of pictures from the same viewpoints. The influence of Monet on Renoir's work is evident.

Nevertheless Manet and Morisot had become very close – Manet's main exhibit at the 1869 Salon shows a moody Berthe on *The Balcony* (*Le Balcon*), for which

MONET
La Grenouillère
oil on canvas
1869. 79 × 60cm
(31 × 24in)
RIGHT

long been a retreat for landscapists such as Corot. Pissarro had meanwhile moved from Pontoise to nearby Louveciennes, where Renoir was staying with him. At a branch of the Seine near Croissy there was a popular floating restaurant and bathing establishment called La Grenouillère (literally "The Froggery") where jaded Parisians would retire on day trips during the summer months to eat, drink, and swim. It was so popular that it was often illustrated in gazettes; the Imperial couple had once stopped there in their boat, adding to its fame. It was here that Renoir and Monet spent much of the summer of 1869.

In yet another begging letter to Bazille from this period Monet also mentions that "I had indeed a dream, a *tableau*, the bathing place at La Grenouillère, for which I have made some rotten sketches . . ." The "rotten sketches" that he and Renoir had been working on that summer were a turning point, they mark the first major examples of the Impressionism to come in the next decade. The conditions were right: the two artists, each working with an eye on the other's canvas, were using paint with an unheard of directness and speed to capture all the elements in view in as unmediated a way as possible. We begin to see in his *Bathers at La Grenouillère* (*Baigneurs à la Grenouillère*) the genesis of Monet's famous advice:

When you go out to paint, try to forget what objects you have before you; a tree, a house, a field or whatever. Merely think here is a little square of blue, here

PISSARRO
The Orchard
oil on canvas
1870. 56.5 × 84cm (22 × 33in)
This painting was created shortly after Pissarro's move to Louveciennes. He worked consistently outdoors during the period, but also kept a studio in Paris. He did not neglect his association with the rest of the Impressionists, regularly attending the meetings at the Café Guerbois.

an oblong of pink, here a streak of yellow, and paint it just as it looks to you, the exact colour and shape, until it gives you your own naïve impression of the scene before you.

Despite the insistence of Monet and Renoir that the Grenouillère paintings were merely *pochades*, or sketches, the distinction between sketch and finished painting was by now becoming blurred. A painting done at La Grenouillère and submitted to the Salon of 1870 (it was rejected and is now lost) appears hardly more "finished" than the *pochades*.

1870–1871: WAR AND THE COMMUNE

In May 1870 the new decade seemed to promise a bright future for the Second Empire. A plebiscite on constitutional changes to establish a cabinet government responsible to parliament was approved by an overwhelming majority of six million. As Cobban describes it, "In the early summer of 1870, though the Empire was in a process of evolution, there seemed not the slightest danger of revolution." By 2nd July the Second Empire was in peril. Following a byzantine and mischievous piece of statecraft on the part of the Prussians, Prince Leopold of Hohenzollern was offered as a candidate for the vacant throne in Spain. France could not tolerate the idea of Prussian involvement within its southern neighbour. The scheme brought back old memories of continual war between the Hapsburg Empire and France. The

Prussians withdrew the offer to Spain ten days later, but this was not satisfactory to Napoleon III and the belligerent Empress Eugénie, a Spaniard, who took it upon herself to demand through the government an assurance from Wilhelm I of Prussia that no more claims would be made to the Spanish throne. The French were looking for the diplomatic victory over Bismarck such an assurance would provide, but they were out-manouevred when on 14th July a provocative telegram arrived from Ems which had been written by Bismarck and calculated to infuriate the French. When the telegram was published in the press, France exploded in patriotic fervour and demanded war with the Prussians. Napoleon III was too ill at the time to resist this tide of emotion and five days later, on 19th July, he was forced to declare war on the Prussians.

By August the French armies had suffered heavy defeats on all fronts. The Prussians' Krupps guns, so admired at the 1867 Exposition Universelle, had been used to devastating effect; the French army was ill equipped, badly led and swiftly demoralized. Napoleon III himself was barely able to sit astride his horse through illness. The Prussians, on the other hand, had built up a formidable war machine under Bismarck, who made use of the railways to transport men and artillery to the fronts; they took Alsace and Lorraine in the first week of fighting. A series of humiliating defeats followed for the French. On 1st September Napoleon III surrendered his army at Sedan and was taken prisoner of

MONET
L'Hôtel des Roches Noires, Trouville oil on canvas 1870. 81 × 58.5cm (32 × 23in)
The Monets were not staying at the luxurious 150-room hotel, but in a modest establishment which they left without paying. The bill was settled much later.

war. Paris erupted in pent-up revolutionary fervour; the Empress Eugénie and the Prince Imperial escaped out of the back door of the Palais de Versailles to England. The chronicler of Parisian life Edmond de Goncourt attempted to describe the chaotic scene as the bad news hit Paris:

> Who can describe the consternation written on every face, the crowds collecting at street corners and outside town halls, the siege of the newspaper kiosks, the triple rows of readers gathering around every gas lamp? Then there is the menacing roar of the crowd in which stupefaction has begun to give way to anger. Next there are crowds moving down the boulevards shouting "*A bas l'Empire!*" ["Down with the Empire!"] . . . And finally there is the wild, tumultuous spectacle of a nation determined to perish or save itself by an enormous effort, by one of those impossible feats of revolutionary times.

A republican government of National Defence was proclaimed by the moderates in the Legislative Assembly. Within three months the Second Empire no longer existed.

On 28th November, a year short of his thirtieth birthday, Frédéric Bazille was killed in battle at Beaunes-la-Rolande near Orléans.

MONET
Beach at Trouville
oil on canvas
1870. 37.5 × 45.5cm
(15 × 18in)
This sketchy picture, an important step on the road to Impressionism, can be compared to an enlarged detail of Boudin's painting of the same subject. The painters were working together that summer, and Mme Boudin is perhaps the other woman in the picture.

MONET
Green Park, London
oil on canvas
1871. 40 × 73cm
(16 × 29in)

One of his last paintings, *Studio in the rue de la Condamine*, depicts some habitués of the Café Guerbois, Monet, Manet, Renoir, Zola, the musician Maître and the artist himself (painted in by Manet) in happier, more peaceful times.

Manet had remained in Paris, a lieutenant in the National Guard under the painter Meissonier. Renoir was sent to Bordeaux, in the southwest and thus saw no action. In Paris Manet was to be seen swanning around in his officer's uniform, although neither he, Renoir, nor Degas were involved in any action. Cézanne had fled back to Aix-en-Provence in the south to avoid being conscripted into a war which was largely being fought in the northeast. Pissarro had painted on in Louveciennes until the Prussians advanced towards it. Over 1,100 of his paintings (which shows how prodigious his output was) were badly damaged or destroyed when his house was commandeered by several enemy troops.

As the war raged in the east Monet was at Trouville painting a number of pictures of the beach and seafront, notably the two *Beach at Trouville* (*La Plage à Trouville*) paintings and *L'Hôtel des Roches Noires, Trouville* which confirm his increasingly impressionistic style. In the autumn, with the Prussians advancing westward to encircle Paris, Monet and Pissarro fled separately to London.

If the war had proved fatal for Bazille, Monet's closest friend and as promising an artist as any of the group, it provided Pissarro and Monet with the opportunity to meet Paul Durand-Ruel, an important dealer who had opened a gallery in London and was later to faithfully champion their work and stage exhibitions of the Impressionists in New York. "A true picture dealer," said Durand-Ruel, "should also be an enlightened patron; he should, if necessary, sacrifice his immediate interest to his artistic convictions and oppose rather than support the interest of speculators." Living in the West End of London, Monet had been introduced to Durand-Ruel by Charles Daubigny, who was making a good living painting scenes of the Thames. Durand-Ruel in turn put Monet in touch with Pissarro who was staying with his mother in South Norwood, a quiet, picturesque village to the southeast of London.

By 20th September 1870 the Prussians had completely surrounded Paris, cutting it off from the rest of France. An attack by the crack Zouaves Regiment had been routed the day before. Edmond de Goncourt heard a terrified national guardsman on the street "relating that the Prussians numbered a hundred thousand in the Bois de Meudon . . . One senses in these accounts the madness of fear, the hallucinations of panic . . ." The Bois de Boulogne had been turned into a farmyard, siege fortifications had been built in and around the city which thronged with soldiers from the National Guard. Throughout the autumn and winter and on into 1871 the war continued, with food supplies running short and starvation becoming rampant.

One of the few links to the outside world was via hot air

PISSARRO

Upper Norwood, Crystal Palace
oil on canvas
1871. 40 × 51cm
(16 × 20in)

This work by Pissarro and the painting opposite by Monet were each the product of the artists' voluntary exile in England during the Franco-Prussian war. It was an important time, as it brought the two men together, but was commercially unsuccessful, as the English public was not yet ready for the Impressionists, and the Royal Academy – equivalent to the French Salon – rejected their work.

PILS
The Ruins of the Tuileries Palace
watercolour on paper
1871. 38 × 51cm (15 × 20in)
ABOVE We have to turn to topographical artists, or to Meissonier, to find pictures of the devastation of war. Most of the Impressionists were out of Paris at the time, and in any case had no desire to paint such scenes.

MANET
Civil War
Lithograph
1871. 40 × 51cm (16 × 20in)
ABOVE The artist had seen corpses lying in the streets near his home.

balloons. On 8th October, Léon Gambetta, a fiery and popular orator and Minister of the Interior, had made an heroic escape to Tours in a balloon launched from the heights of Montmartre. Taking advantage of this, Nadar organized letters to be sent by balloon post. One letter from Berthe Morisot to her sister, Edma, describes the noise of the Prussian bombardments which began in November, the corpses lying in the streets and grim warnings from Edouard and Eugène Manet that Berthe would be better off if she lost her hand or became disfigured. On 19th January the Paris garrison attempted to break out of the city and through the Prussian lines, but failed. This attempted *sortie en masse* was the last significant action of the war. Nine days later Paris surrendered to the Prussian army.

In February a republican National Assembly was elected to make peace with Prussia and approve massive reparations. But the National Guard was still armed in Paris and when on 18th March troops loyal to the new republican government attempted and failed to seize the cannon in Montmartre, Paris – led by a coalition of revolutionaries – was at war with the Republic. On 28th March the Paris Commune was elected amid scenes of jubilation that harked back to the days of the Revolution in 1789 and the first Commune. On 2nd April the second siege of Paris began; the Commune held out until the "Bloody Week" which began on 21st May when more than 20,000 Parisians were killed in

indiscriminate reprisals as government forces overran the city.

Gustave Courbet, who had been elected chairman of the Arts Commission after the fall of the Empire, was a prominent member of the Commune and became implicated in the destruction of the Vendôme Column, which stood as a bitter reminder of Napoleonic power to the Communards. When the government "liberated" Paris he was imprisoned and later exiled to Switzerland where he died in 1877.

Amidst the dramatic events of this period Degas' eyesight had begun to deteriorate, Renoir had obtained a pass during the Commune and left to continue his landscape studies and most of the others of the Batignolles Group had fled to safety.

Manet was the only member of the group concerned with depicting the war in Paris and its effects. Standing on the corner of the boulevard Malesherbes, he sketched the dead bodies lying there.

The lithograph *The Civil War* (*La Guerre civile*) shows how readily his *Execution of Maximilian* must have come to his mind as he observed the horror in the streets of Paris at that perilous time: the starvation, sheer anarchy, and devastation.

DEGAS IN NEW ORLEANS

For illustrations of the Commune we have to turn to photography and the topographic artists who remained in Paris to record the suffering and destruction. None of the Impressionists was interested in the ruins of the Tuileries Palace, which had stood in the heart of the city, an area they had often depicted before the war.

In the end, the war against Prussia and the Commune had little effect on the French economy. France was now a *de facto* republic for the third time in her history. In the climate of expansion which immediately followed the end of the troubles Durand-Ruel began to invest heavily in the Batignolles artists. He bought 30 Monets and paid Manet 51,000 francs for 29 of his paintings, a fantastic sum considering Claude Monet's income the next year was 25,000 francs. For Monet in particular things were looking up at last. From England he had gone to Holland and then to Argenteuil on the Seine near Paris where Renoir frequently joined him as before. Pissarro had returned to Louveciennes and then decamped to Pontoise where Cézanne visited him. The Café Guerbois evenings continued for another year. In November Degas and his brother René arrived in New Orleans to stay with their mother. In a letter to his friend Lorentz Fröhlich, Degas described the effect the new world was having on him:

Everything attracts me here, I look at everything . . . I accumulate plans that would take a lifetime to complete. I will abandon them in six weeks to return and never again leave my home . . . My eyes are much better.

Ten days later he wrote to Henri Rouart:

The light is so strong that I have not yet been able to do anything on the river. My eyes are so greatly in need of care that I scarcely take any risk with them at all . . . Manet would see lovely things here, even more than I do . . .

Indicative of his friendly rivalry with Manet he went on:

. . . but not many more of them. One loves and gives art only to the things to which one is accustomed.

Among the results of Degas' period in New Orleans, chiefly devoted to painting portraits of his family, are two remarkable pictures, *The Invalid* (*L'Invalide*) and *Portraits in an Office – New Orleans* (*Portraits dans un bureau à Nouvelle-Orléans*) better known as *The Cotton Market* (*Le Bureau de Coton*). The former is one of Degas' most atmospheric works, conveying what Henri Loyrette calls "the stifling sense of the

PISSARRO
Horsechestnut Trees at Louveciennes
oil on canvas
c.1872. 41 × 54cm (16 × 21in)
This evocative snow-scene was painted close to the artist's home at Louveciennes, where he had moved with his family three years before.

MANET
The Railway
1872–73.
93.5 × 114.5cm
(37 × 45in)
Also called The Gare St Lazare, *we can hardly guess that there is a railway station behind the cloud of smoke. Most Impressionists painted scenes with trains at this time.*

sickroom" in broad, swift brushstrokes; the latter, making the modern business world a legitimate subject for art, was described by Armand Silvestre as "an exceedingly witty painting that one could spend days contemplating." This painting is perhaps as epochal as Manet's *Music in the Tuileries Garden* had been a decade earlier. After this Degas' failing eyes allowed him to paint few pictures of such acute detail.

1873: SOCIÉTÉ ANONYME

The post-war boom soon gave way to a period of economic recession which lasted for five years and affected the Impressionists, their patrons, and especially Durand-Ruel, forcing him to close his London gallery in 1874. As in 1863 the Salon was hugely oversubscribed but this time the refusés succeeded in pressurizing the government to mount another

Salon des Refusés. A huge Renoir painting, almost eight and a half by seven and a half feet, the *Morning Ride in the Bois de Boulogne* (*Allée cavalière au Bois de Boulogne*) had been rejected by the Salon but was shown to great acclaim at the alternative exhibition.

Monet's influence on Renoir, after long months working with him before and after the war, had led to a brightening of his palette and more delicate brushwork. Renoir's *Pont Neuf* of the previous year was one of his most impressionistic pictures to date; the briefly sketched-in figures highlighted with dabs of pure pigment betray the influence of Monet, as do the complementary colours blue-violet and yellow in the overall composition, and the bluish shadows, which create the effect of colour contrast in brilliant sunlight.

Unlike the events a decade earlier, the Salon des Refusés of 1873 was remarkably devoid of scandal. The painter most likely to cause an uproar, Edouard Manet, was showing two works at the official Salon, a portrait of Berthe Morisot and *Le Bon Bock* – a portrait of the engraver Bellot at a table in the Café Guerbois. The latter proved a welcome success for Manet, sensitive as ever to the barbs of the critics. The influence of Frans Hals, whom Manet had been studying during a tour of Holland the year before, as well as the deliberate lack of a scandalous subject gently reassured the Salon-going public of Manet's talent.

The Salon des Refusés did little to placate the rest of the Batignolles Group who were still desperately looking for outlets for their work. Ironically, the war had promoted a deeply conservative streak in the Salon jury which made Nieuwerkerke's *ancien régime* appear liberal by comparison. This conspired against an avant-garde whose influence was by now becoming widespread. With Durand-Ruel's business suffering in the recession and unable to support them they were forced to look elsewhere. The idea first mentioned by Bazille in 1867 of forming an independent organization to stage an exhibition was rekindled. A much heated discussion between Pissarro, who was for a highly complex association based on a social and political union, and the others in the group, including Renoir and Monet, who demanded a simpler, looser collective, resulted in a document signed on 27th December founding the *Société anonyme des artistes peintres, sculpteurs, graveurs, etc.* Only Manet refused to join the new body, arguing in common with Cézanne, that still "the Salon is the true battlefield." Degas was in favour, writing to Tissot that "the realist movement no longer needs to fight with the others. It is. It exists, it must show itself as something distinct . . . So forget the money side for a moment. Exhibit. Be of your country and your friends."

SISLEY
The Seine at Bougival
oil on canvas 1872–77.
38.5 × 62cm (15 × 24in)
Sisley was interested at this time in the problems of depicting water and sky. His palette was somewhat dark and sombre compared to most of the other Impressionists.

THE AGE OF IMPRESSIONISM

THE WORKS OF MONET, Renoir, Manet, Morisot, Pissarro and Sisley, which characterized the Impressionist idiom in its most popularly recognizable form, were painted in the 1870s. Degas, who played an important role in organizing the series of Impressionist exhibitions which marked the 1870s and 1880s, remained resolutely opposed to *plein-air* painting. He nevertheless produced the most striking images of modern Parisian life, taking inspiration from Japanese prints and photography, and, like Manet, basing his technique on a thorough appreciation of the old masters. Towards the end of the 1870s serious rifts began to appear in the group and Monet, Renoir, and Sisley dropped out as Degas and Pissarro exerted more and more control over the exhibitions, replenishing the group with new artists. For most of the Impressionists this was a time of personal consolidation, with patrons and dealers securing them a regular income despite periodic economic recessions. The penultimate Impressionist exhibition – minus Degas – took place in 1882 and essentially represented the fragile group's last stand. The next year Manet died having completed his masterpiece *Bar at the Folies-Bergère*. He had remained highly supportive of the group but never exhibited with them.

By 1886 the final Impressionist exhibition featured the work of Degas, Pissarro, and a new generation including Georges Seurat, Paul Signac, and Paul Gauguin.

MONET
The Sea at Fécamp (DETAIL) oil on canvas 1881. 65 × 80cm (26 × 32in)

1874: THE FIRST IMPRESSIONIST EXHIBITION

*We were all one group when we first started out. We stood
shoulder to shoulder and encouraged each other . . .*

The quotation above was given by Renoir, twenty years after the inaugural collective Impressionist show: the *Société anonyme's* first (and last) exhibition opened in mid-April, deliberately timed to upstage the official Salon. Situated in Nadar's old studio, it was close to the premises of several dealers and photographers, including Durand-Ruel's gallery. The choice of a *grand boulevard* was in itself a fitting one for the generation of artists who had grown up in Haussmann's Paris painting Baudelaire's *vie moderne*.

The exhibition was immediately a critical *cause célèbre*; not only did it provoke the aspersions of critics such as Leroy, it also rallied the influential theorist Edmond Duranty (with whom Manet had once fought a duel!) to the Impressionists' defence. At the time, Jules Castagnary also showed particular insight in putting his finger on the fact that Monet,

MILLET
Haystacks in Autumn
oil on canvas
1873–74. 85 × 110cm
(34 × 43in)
Though charmingly done in their own right, Millet's haystacks are perhaps of more interest through their very obvious foreshadowing of the magnificent series by Monet.

Pissarro, Sisley, Morisot, and Renoir were "Impressionists in the sense that they render not the landscape, but the sensation produced by the landscape."

However, the exhibition was such a financial disaster that the *Société* was later forced to meet in December to wind up its affairs. Thanks to Louis Leroy's scurrilous satire in *Charivari*, the group, which had laboured under several titles, none of them really appropriate – *la bande à Manet*, the Batignolles Group, the Realists – was now known as "the Impressionists". There were seven more Impressionist exhibitions, the last in 1886, although none of them bore the title "Impressionist", their participants typically preferring the name *Expositions de Peinture*, or on one occasion, an *Exposition des Independants*.

All but forgotten in a new world of painting, Charles Gleyre died that same year. Renoir, for one, maintained to the very end that Gleyre had taught him his *métier*. He recalled a scene at Gleyre's a decade before:

Whilst the other students yelled and broke the windows, tormented the model and distracted the teacher I would quietly sit in the corner, observant and prepared, studying the model and listening to the master. And they accused me of being a revolutionary.

1875: CRITICS AND COLLECTORS

The Salon of 1875 was graced with the results of Edouard Manet's work at Argenteuil where he had spent the previous summer with Monet and Renoir. Manet had helped Monet's family to find new lodgings in this picturesque village on the banks of the Seine and proceeded under the latter's influence to create a series of highly impressionistic figures in landscapes. Liberated from the studio and surrounded by the most devoted of Impressionist *plein-airistes*, Manet's technique underwent a revolution. *Monet Painting in his Studio Boat* (*Monet dans son studio flotant*), *Banks of the Seine at Argenteuil* (*Les Bords de la Seine à Argenteuil*) (the two figures are Camille Monet and Jean), and *The Monet Family in their Garden*

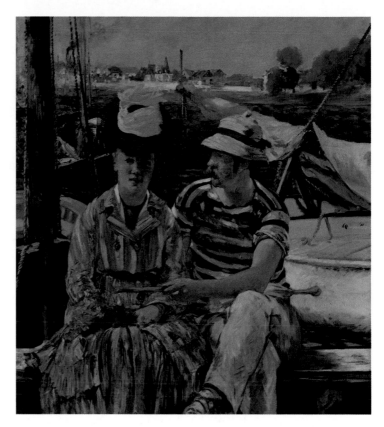

MANET
Banks of the Seine at Argenteuil
oil on canvas
1874. 148 × 115cm (58 × 45in)
Manet's technique shows the liberating influence of Monet and Renoir; his palette is brighter than ever and his style is at last truly impressionistic.

BOUDIN
Beach Scene, Trouville
oil on canvas
1873. 15 × 30cm (6 × 12in)
*One of many scenes of this
kind by Boudin. He deplored the
invasion of tourists but could
not avoid depicting them. Boudin
flirted with Impressionism, and
indeed his work was included in
the first Impressionist exhibition.
Yet he was a free spirit, refusing
to permanently ally himself
to any specific grouping.*

(*La Famille Monet au jardin*) are remarkable for the breathtaking speed of their execution and the abandonment of Manet's otherwise sombre palette in favour of strokes of pure pigment. The contrast between Monet's insistence on landscape as his *motif* – his reluctance to attempt large figures after *Women in the Garden* some ten years earlier is palpable – and Manet's abiding concern with the human figure is still marked, even at the point where their styles most obviously converge.

The respite offered by Durand-Ruel to the poorest Impressionists, Monet, Renoir, Pissarro, and Sisley (whose father's business had collapsed in the war) had temporarily evaporated; sales had plummeted in the recession. Even Degas was in trouble after the death of his father had entailed the Degas estate. An auction of Impressionist work arranged by Renoir and held at the

Hôtel Drouot ended in farce and near riot. So derisory were the bids that the artists were forced to purchase many of their own works. Albert Wolff, the art critic of the important daily *Le Figaro*, had been asked by Manet to promote the sale. His answer was to write "the impression the Impressionists achieve [is] that of a cat walking on a piano keyboard or a monkey who might have got hold of a box of paints."

Gradually, however, patrons were beginning to come to the aid of some of the Impressionists. An eccentric customs official called Victor Chocquet, who had devoted his life to collecting the work of Delacroix and many other objets d'art, had become enamoured of Renoir's work at the Hôtel Drouot and began to support the Impressionists. Renoir introduced him to Cézanne, also in need of more patronage and the result was a series of portraits of M. and Mme Chocquet by the two artists. A comparison of Renoir's and Cézanne's 1876 portraits of the collector shows the difference in the two artists' approach to their subject. Renoir's picture is executed with feathery brush strokes evoking a gentle, kindly, almost ethereal individual; Cézanne's portrait (like the later portrait of 1879–82) shows his increasing concern with structure and volume, and the paint is applied in thick patches and with the palette knife.

The second Impressionist exhibition planned for 1875 was unable to go ahead because there were no available funds to mount it. Although this decline of the *Société anonyme* was only a temporary set-back, some serious rifts were already beginning to appear in the group. In August Pissarro and his

GUILLAUMIN
The Aqueduct at Arcueil
oil on canvas
1874. 51 × 65cm (20 × 26in)
Among the Impressionists, Guillaumin was one of the few to depict the grim aspects of the urban industrial landscape.

friend Alfred Meyer set up *L'Union* to carry on the work of the defunct *Société anonyme*. Cézanne and Monet objected to this upstart organization, especially the involvement of Meyer who they believed was plotting against the artistic objectives of the Impressionists. Although *L'Union* had recruited several minor painters to its ranks, including Guillaumin, it attracted little attention from the critics and eventually faded into oblivion. However much this singular group of artists was identified by the critics, the public and other artists as a homogenous circle their talents and personalities were formidably individual. A mutual struggle against the inflexibility of the art world brought them "shoulder to shoulder", but that alone was not enough to keep the Impressionists together for very much longer.

The death of Camille Corot in 1875, the inspiration for so many of the Impressionists, was an occasion for much sadness in the group, especially for Berthe Morisot and Camille Pissarro who had been closest to him and learned the most from his work and artistic guidance. "We don't see in the same way; you see green and I see grey and silver," Corot once said to Pissarro, ". . . but this is no reason at all for you not to work at [tonal] values, for this is the basis of everything, and in whatever way one may feel and express oneself, one cannot do good painting without it." Morisot had outgrown Corot's style by the time of the first Impressionist exhibition, as her painting *The Cradle* (*Berceau*) indicates, but Corot's influence on Pissarro persisted well into the 1870s.

PHOTOGRAPHY AND IMPRESSIONISM

Of great interest to art historians is the fact that over three hundred photographs were found in Corot's studio after his death. These photographs are now lost, but a contemporary source described two hundred of them as being "studies from nature".

The first reliable photographic process had been discovered by Louis Daguerre and announced to the French Académie des Sciences in 1839. (In 1822 Joseph-Nicéphore Niepce had succeeded in fixing a photographic image on glass, and William Henry Fox Talbot in England was developing a rival process which could reproduce from negatives.) The daguerreotype was capable of producing a positive image fixed on a highly polished metal plate and soon became widely available. The new invention had an immediate effect on artists, especially miniature portrait painters: it put many of them out of business. Nevertheless the practical applications of the new medium were apparent to major artists such as Ingres and Delacroix. The latter made no secret of his admiration, a daguerreotype, he said:

> . . . is a mirror of the object, certain details, almost always neglected in drawings from nature . . . in the daguerreotype take on a great importance and bring the artist into a full understanding of the object's construction. There, passages of light and shade show their true qualities . . .

In fact the daguerreotype was often more prone to distorting reality.

MANET
Masked Ball at the Opera
oil on canvas
1873–74. 60 × 73cm (24 × 29in)

*On the left, talking to a masked woman
in white, is the composer Chabrier,
a friend of several Impressionists.
This kind of entertainment was not
suitable for the respectable Mme Manet
or Berthe Morisot.*

MORISOT
Chasing Butterflies
oil on canvas
1874. 47 × 56cm (19 × 22in)
ABOVE Morisot had work accepted by the official Salon as early as 1864, when she was only twenty-three, but it was not until 1879, five years after their inaugural exhibition, that she first showed with the Impressionists.

Very slow exposure speeds in the 1850s meant that gently moving objects like trees were recorded on the plate in a blurred image, the light from the sky eating into the moving edges of the foliage. Corot and the Barbizon School were closely acquainted with the landscape photographers of the time who, as the historian of photography Aaron Scharf suggests, must have been setting up their tripods right next to the painters' easels in the leafy recesses of the Fontainebleau Forest and in other landscape sites. After 1840 there is increasing and direct use of the "halated" or blurred effect in the outline of Corot's trees as well as the influence of photographic over- and underexposure in his astute handling of light and dark areas.

By the 1860s "snapshots" with fast exposure times were possible and Talbot's system of producing copies on paper from a negative had made the photograph widely available. Manet's *The Execution of The Emperor Maximilian*

CASSATT
On the Balcony
oil on canvas 1873.
101 × 83cm (40 × 33in) *RIGHT*

(*L'Execution de l'empereur Maximilien*) is partly indebted to photographs taken in Mexico of the doomed Emperor and his aides. As a cultural expression of its time, *The Execution* stands poised between the instantaneous modernity of the photograph with its ability to capture current events, and the art of Goya who had painted his *Third of May* (1808) in the first Napoleonic era.

Describing Monet's painting in 1874 Ernest Chesneau perceptively wrote: "Never has the elusive, the fleeting, the instantaneous movement been caught in its incredible flux and fixed, as it is in this extraordinary *Boulevard des Capucines*." The previously unseen, blurred forms of moving people and objects which the camera could reveal had now become part of the vocabulary of the Impressionists, whether or not the influence was a conscious one.

In the year Corot died Degas painted the *Place de la Concorde* (now sadly lost). Of his contemporaries it was Degas who exploited the photograph to its fullest potential, later using it to help him with studies of dancers and horses. The view of the *Place de la Concorde* with the Vicomte Lepic and his daughters frozen in motion, sliced off by the bottom of the picture, and an onlooker on the left similarly clipped by the frame, is clearly reminiscent of a snapshot and influenced by the new ways of framing made possible by the camera.

MONET
Boulevard des Capucines
oil on canvas
1873–74. 79 × 59cm (31 × 23in)
BELOW This picture was painted in the autumn from Nadar's old photographic studio on the second floor. The brand-new Grand Hotel is on the left.

MONET
Impression, Sunrise
oil on canvas
1872. 48 × 63cm (19 × 25in)
*ABOVE This is the painting that
provoked Leroy into coining the
name Impressionism at the group's
first joint exhibition in 1874.*

1876–1877: LA NOUVELLE
PEINTURE

"None of its members show signs
of possessing first-rate talent, and
indeed the 'Impressionist' doctrines
strike me as incompatible, in an
artist's mind, with the existence of
first-rate talent. To embrace them
you must be provided with a
plentiful absence of imagination."

HENRY JAMES,
THE NEW YORK TRIBUNE
13TH MAY 1876.

PISSARRO
La Côte du Chou, Pontoise
oil on canvas
c.1875–76. 81.5 × 65cm
(32 × 26in)
*RIGHT At this stage of his career
Pissarro was increasingly being
sought out by his younger
Impressionist colleagues for help
and advice. Cézanne, in particular,
was a frequent visitor to Pontoise
(where Pissarro and his family had
returned in 1872), and once said
that his friend was "a little like the
good Lord."*

The second Impressionist exhibition opened in mid-April 1876 at Durand-Ruel's gallery in the rue Le Pelletier. Some of the more extreme critics had seized the opportunity of likening the group to madmen and syphilitics, so Henry James's criticism seems mild by comparison. Yet it was typical of the prevailing school of thought which still could not accept Impressionism in any form. A critical defence was needed and several writers sympathetic to the Impressionists came to their aid. In his pamphlet *La Nouvelle Peinture*, Edmond Duranty analysed the "new painting" in some depth. Monet, Renoir, and Pissarro were less than pleased with Duranty's tacit praise of Degas at their expense, but *La Nouvelle Peinture* offers some thoughtful insights into the Impressionists' work. This is what he had to say about the Impressionist use of colour:

> Their real discovery consists in the realization that a strong light *discolours* tones, that sunshine reflected off objects tends by virtue of its clarity to blend its seven prismatic rays into a single, uncoloured brilliance which is light. From one flash of intuition to another, they have succeeded in breaking up solar light into its rays, its elements, and to reconstruct it as a unity by the general harmony of the iridescence they spread on their canvases. From the viewpoint of the refinement of vision and the subtle penetration of colours, it has produced an extraordinary result. The most astute physicist could find no fault with their analysis of colour.

Other critics did not agree. One of the fifteen works by Renoir at the second exhibition (several were on loan from Victor Chocquet) was the *Étude*, better known as *Nude in Sunlight*. In his satire on the first exhibition Leroy had conceded that the painter "has a certain understanding of colour"; and Silvestre in *L'Opinion* thought *Nude in Sunlight* "the work of a true colourist." Wolff, however, in *Le Figaro* made a devastating attack focused on Renoir's palette:

> Would someone kindly explain to M. Renoir that a woman's torso is not a mass of decomposing flesh with the green and purplish blotch-es that indicate a state of complete putrefaction in a corpse ...

Not to be outdone in similes of corrupt flesh, Louis Enault in *Le Constitutionnel* offered his readers this opinion:

> It is depressing to look at this large study of a nude woman; her purplish flesh is the colour of game that has been hung for too long, and someone really should have made her put on a dress.

Despite these attacks this was, as art historian Phoebe Pool says, Renoir's *annus mirabilis*. Not only do two of his finest paintings, *The Swing (La Balançoire)* and the *Ball at the Moulin de la Galette (Bal du Moulin de la Galette)*, date from this period, but he had the good fortune to meet Georges Charpentier, a wealthy young publisher who became an important patron. Mme Charpentier's salon was an

RENOIR
The Greenhouse
oil on canvas
Undated. 60 × 74cm (24 × 29in)
RIGHT

MONET
The Seine at Vétheuil
oil on canvas
1879. 60 × 81cm
(24 × 32in)
*This picture was painted during
a period when Monet's fortunes
were at a very low ebb, but
personal or financial difficulties
never did affect his incredible
work-rate.*

important meeting place for the intellectual and social élite of the day. Renoir's later portrait of Mme Charpentier is described by Proust in *Time Regained* (*Le Temps retrouvé*) as being comparable to the best of Titian.

It was also around this time that a young painter of independent means, Gustave Caillebotte, became an important force amongst the Impressionists. His *Floor Scrapers* (*Les Raboteurs de parquets*) and *Le Pont de l'Europe* were shown at the second Impressionist exhibition. The influence of Degas and photography is discernible in the deep perspective, and whilst the style can hardly be called "impressionistic" in the sense of Monet, Sisley, or Renoir, these and several later paintings, notably the *Boulevard Seen from Above* (*Boulevard vu d'en haut*) have often been mentioned as some of the most memorable urban images of his century. Seven years younger than Renoir and Monet, Caillebotte was soon engaged in organizing the 1877 exhibition and funding the group through the extensive purchase of some of their most important works, with the intention of bequeathing them to the State. (There were sixty in all, including the two by Renoir mentioned above, now in the Musée d'Orsay, in Paris).

As Renoir's fortunes waxed for the time being, Monet's waned. During the years between 1876 and 1880 Monet was consistently forced to rely on the largesse of others. He described himself as being penniless and destitute, although he was still earning (and spending) six times more than the average workman whilst occasionally living in some style. Nevertheless the third Impressionist exhibition held at Durand-Ruel's and funded by Caillebotte, showed that penury could not stop Monet's outflow of work.

In January Caillebotte had rented a small apartment and studio for Monet close to the Gare St Lazare, the main station for points west of Paris, including the Normandy coast, Argenteuil, and Bougival (in 1877 it handled 13 million passengers). With the sort of bravado only a penniless artist like Monet could summon up, he went to call on the Superintendent of the railway who assumed him to be a famous artist and offered him the freedom of the station. A series of twelve paintings was the result, seven of which were shown at the third exhibition. Greeted with astonishment, they proved to be the last of his urban landscapes. Georges Rivière, an art critic of the time held the overall view that "these paintings are amazingly varied, despite the monotony and aridity of the subject. In them more than anywhere else can be seen that skill in arrangement, that organization of the canvas, that is one of the main qualities of Monet's work." Trains and the new railways were indeed an important feature in the work of the other artists, notably Pissarro, Sisley, and Manet. Manet's *The Railway* (*Le Chemin de fer*) of 1873 tells us a great deal about the difference between him and Monet. It is primarily a figure painting: the railway itself is beyond the picture and represented by a cloud of steam; the little girl stands (like Degas' double-bass) with her back to us. Manet, unlike Monet, is not primarily interested in the railway as such, but in the relationship between it and his figures. As an icon of its time it is a powerful image, portraying a sense of wonderment (the girl) and banality (the woman) in the modern world.

Looking at this modern world from an entirely different perspective, Degas' contribution to the exhibition included two celebrated images of Parisian vice; *In a Café* (also known as *The Absinthe Drinker*) and *Women on the Terrace of a Café in the Evening* (*Femmes à la terrasse d'un café soir*). Of the latter, the contemporary critic Alexandre Pothey confessed,

MONET
Gare St Lazare, Pont de l'Europe
oil on canvas
1877. 64 × 81cm
(25 × 32in)
The railway bridge seen at train level, a much more animated and interesting composition than Caillebotte's work.

MONET
Gare St Lazare
oil on canvas
1877. 60 × 80cm
(24 × 32in)
*ABOVE Monet put on his best suit,
went to the director of railways
and asked permission to paint
inside the station. Mistaken
for a famous artist, the station
was cleared for him, the engines
stacked to provide abundant
smoke, and he was escorted by
railway officials. He painted
twelve views of the station and
showed seven of them at the third
Impressionist show of 1877.*

MONET
The Japanese Kimono
oil on canvas
1876. 231 × 142cm
(91 × 56in)
*ABOVE RIGHT The model is Monet's
first wife, Camille.*

DEGAS
Three studies for a
Fourteen-year-old Dancer
chalk and charcoal on green paper
c.1876–80. 48 × 63cm
(19 × 25in)
*RIGHT The exhaustive studies for this
sculpture demonstrate both Degas'
determination to master his subject
completely, and his cautious move into
a new medium, that of sculpture, which
became increasingly important in later
years when his eyesight began to fail.*

"the terrifying realism of these painted, faded creatures, exuding vice, who cynically tell each other about their day's activities and accomplishments." The scandal caused by Manet's *Olympia* twelve years before in the long summer days of the Second Empire had been instrumental in clearing the way for Degas' explicit depiction of prostitution and alcoholism, now tacitly acceptable in polite Third Republic society. If Baudelaire had survived he would have been delighted, for Degas was now the painter of modern life *par excellence*, making art of everything that went on in Paris, from the loneliest bar to the heaving café-concert. His interest in ballet had resulted in *The Star (L'Etoile)* and *Dancers at the Barre*, whilst the café-concert, a sort of vaudeville or music hall at the height of its popularity in the 1870s, was the trigger for several pictures on this subject, as indeed it was for Renoir and Manet.

DEGAS
The Star
pastel/monotype
c.1878. 60 × 44cm
(24 × 17in)
*RIGHT Degas said, "People call me the
painter of dancing girls. It has never
occurred to them that my chief interest
in dancers lies in rendering movement
and in painting pretty clothes."*

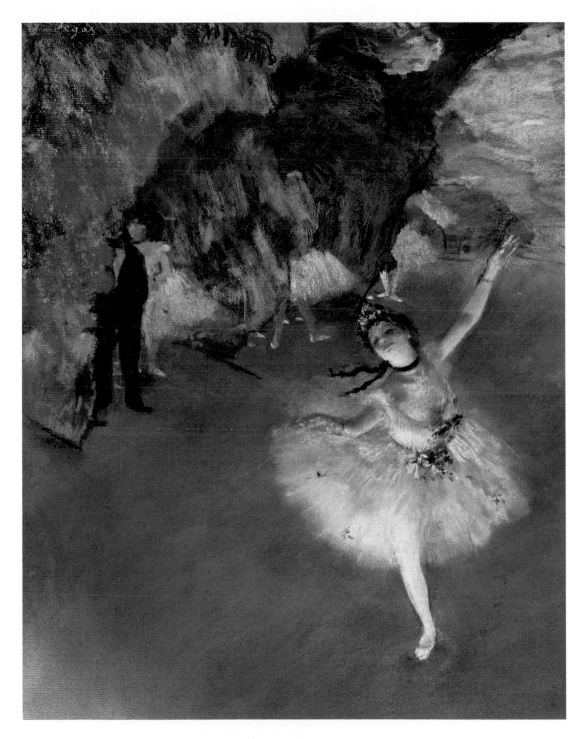

1878–1881: BEGINNING OF THE END

We are far from the moment when we are able to do without the prestige attached to the official exhibitions.

ALFRED SISLEY, 1878

In 1878 an important patron of the Impressionists, Ernest Hoschedé, the director of a Paris department store, was in serious financial difficulties which later forced him to sell a sizeable collection of works he had accumulated after the first Impressionist exhibition in 1874. Monet in particular was affected by the impending fall of Hoschedé; he had made extensive use of Hoschedé's country house at Montgeron near Paris and had produced some important work for the collector. The loss of a patron was bad enough; Monet and Camille now had a second child to support, they had recently been forced to leave their house in Argenteuil, relying on Edouard Manet to find them lodgings at Lavacourt near Vétheuil, a village over thirty miles from Paris. The Monets were already desperate, as Camille was ill with cancer of the uterus, and to make things worse, the Hoschedés were ruined, and they came, with their six children, to stay. To complicate matters Claude had been having a secret liaison with Hoschedé's wife, Alice, for some time. Thus began a strange *ménage à douze*. From around this time Monet began to be more and more isolated from the other Impressionists, rarely venturing into Paris.

One of the founding members of the *Société anonyme* who had already cut himself off from the group to a certain extent, pursuing his own aims and methods, was Alfred Sisley. He was becoming a recluse; some years later he crossed the street to avoid Renoir who had once been one of his closest friends. Eight years earlier Sisley's father's business had crashed during the Franco-Prussian War and from this time to his death in 1899 his life was a continual struggle to support his family. His finest work dates from the mid-1870s. Sisley had lived near Argenteuil in the earlier part of the decade and between 1875 and 1877 he had gone to Marly-le-Roi to continue his landscapes. In 1878 he got his work into the Salon along with Renoir; both artists had now officially left the Impressionists. Sisley told Duret that:

It is true that our exhibitions have served to make us known and in this they have been very useful to me, but I believe we must not isolate ourselves for too long. We are far from the moment when we are able to do without the prestige attached to the official exhibitions. I am therefore determined to submit to the Salon.

DEGAS
Women on the Terrace of a Café
in the Evening
pastel/monotype
1877. 41 × 60cm (16 × 24in)

PISSARRO
The Kitchen Garden
oil on canvas
1879. 55 × 65cm
(22 × 26in)
Whereas Renoir had a longing to be accepted by high society, Pissarro remained staunchly loyal to his principles and continued to paint humble subjects.

Underlying this dissatisfaction was the increasing dominance that Degas (and Caillebotte) seemed to be exerting on the group. A benign example of Degas' influence can be seen in his patronage of a young American, Mary Cassatt, who had been living in France since 1866 and had shown twice at the Salon. But other, lesser artists were now to be drafted into the Impressionist exhibitions to make up for the loss of Renoir, Sisley, and later Monet himself. Clearly the Impressionist exhibitions had partially succeeded in promulgating the "movement" but the Impressionists themselves could not expect to live on the proceeds. Chocquet, Charpentier, and other patrons (Manet and Caillebotte also

fulfilled this role) were still vital to their livelihood, and, as frustration with the relative failure of the independent shows grew, Renoir, Sisley, and Monet in particular looked once again to the Salon. The radical Pissarro would not countenance this and in 1878, a year when there was no Impressionist exhibition, he rented a room in the Montmartre quarter of Paris to exhibit his own pictures, which were ironically less radical than ever before, to potential clients. Pissarro, like Monet, had recently lost a friend and patron, Ludovic Piette, a landscapist of some talent who had exhibited with the Impressionists and had died in 1877, depriving Pissarro of an important source of income.

"A BANAL SCHOOL"

The fourth Impressionist exhibition opened on 10th April 1879 at 28 avenue de l'Opéra in Paris without Sisley, Renoir, Morisot (who was pregnant) and Cézanne, but it had works by Cassatt, Forain, Zandomeneghi (all protégés of Degas) and an as yet unknown painter by the name of Paul Gauguin, who had been befriended by Pissarro. For once it was a success and the irony was that as the crowds flocked to see the exhibition there were precious few of the major Impressionists on view. The Salon was now the place to see works like Renoir's *Portrait of Madame Charpentier and Her Children* (*Madame Charpentier et ses enfants*) and Manet's *Boating* (*En Bateau*), both of which received considerable acclaim. That April Georges Charpentier published the first edition of *La Vie Moderne*, a magazine of style, science, comment, and criticism aimed at the well-to-do Parisian. *La Vie Moderne* instituted a series of exhibitions at which Renoir in 1879, and Manet and Monet in 1880, were to have hugely successful one-man shows. As Monet's work finally began to receive the praise he had longed for he was at his most isolated, declaring, "I am still and always intend to be an Impressionist – but very rarely see the men and women who are my colleagues. The little church has become a banal school which opens its doors to the first dauber that comes along."

MANET
At the Père Lathuille
oil on canvas
1879. 93 × 112cm
(37 × 44in)
The Impressionists challenged not only the technique but also the subject matter of the academic style as taught in the Ecole. Manet, although not radically different in technique, turned his eye away from the traditional, classical content of painting by depicting the modern life of Paris. Here he has chosen a restaurant in the Batignolles area near where he lived as the setting for what could have been an ordinarily bourgeois scene.

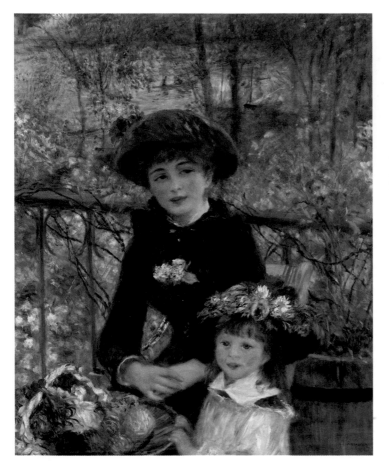

RENOIR
The Terrace
oil on canvas
1881. 100 × 81cm
(39 × 32in)
*LEFT Renoir was still painting
landscapes, but portraits were
a favourite subject.*

believed, which was steadily paralysing him. His appearance with the others would have been a fitting conclusion to a decade he had spent devoted to them. Nevertheless his last great masterpiece, *A Bar at the Folies-Bergère* (*Le Bar aux Folies-Bergère*) was shown at the Salon of 1882 as he received for the last time the official recognition he so desperately desired.

The painting can perhaps be seen as a summation of his adventure as a "painter of modern life". It shows a barmaid, blank-faced, before a mirror reflecting the incessant nightlife of Paris; there is an improbable reflection of her and her customer to the right which touches the borders of surrealism: we might be that customer. In the top left hand corner the legs of an acrobat are bizarrely severed by the frame. A moment of staggering insignificance captured in the very heart of the City of Light.

Manet died on 30th April 1883, at the age of fifty-one. A sale of his work in 1884 realized the modest sum of 116,637 francs for 167 paintings, an average of less than 700 francs per work, far below anything paid for an official Salon painting, or even the Barbizon School which had now become highly collectable.

GAUGUIN
The Sculptor Abbi and His Son
oil on canvas
1882. 53 × 71cm (21 × 28in)
BELOW

penultimate exhibition in the rue Saint-Honoré. Although there was to be another show in 1886, this was in reality their last stand. For a final time, and with great difficulty, Caillebotte and Pissarro (with the aid of Durand-Ruel) had gathered together the work of Monet, Morisot, Renoir, and Sisley (with Gauguin, Guillaumin, and Vignon) under one roof. At the last moment Edouard Manet was struck with indecision about whether to join the group. At any rate he was now in the final stages of his illness, a form of locomotor ataxia it is

1883–1886: THE LAST SHOW

Renoir was in the throes of a crisis: "I had come to the end of Impressionism. I was reaching the conclusion that I didn't know how either to paint or draw. In a word, I was at a dead end." In 1882 he had been travelling in Italy and Sicily where he had painted a portrait of Richard Wagner; from there he had joined Cézanne at l'Estaque on the Côte d'Azur and fell seriously ill with pneumonia. His journey to Italy was mainly a quest for classical art and technique. He studied the wall paintings of Pompeii and even more so the perfect smoothness of Raphael's works in Rome, which led him to work in a tighter, more refined and precise style for a while, before he returned to his instinctive, less disciplined brushwork. The conflict of his styles heightened a personal and artistic crisis which is eloquently demonstrated in his painting *The Umbrellas* (*Les Parapluies*), reworked during the 1880s and left unfinished. Cézanne's powerful influence is evident in Renoir's solid handling of the umbrellas; the

MONET
The Cliffs at Varengeville
oil on canvas
1882.
A favourite subject for Monet, the cliffs along the Normandy coast provided him with a spectacular mixture of land- and seascape.

THE LIFE
AND WORKS

T

ALENTED ARTISTS as diverse as Gauguin, Cassatt, and Cézanne held Camille Pissarro in the utmost reverence as a teacher and a man of integrity. His selfless devotion to the cause of art and his fellow artists endeared him in a way that few, if any, of his contemporaries could claim. His openness enabled him to transcend his (at best theoretical) anarchist convictions and get on with the likes of the extremely reactionary Degas and the innately conservative Renoir, whilst he was a natural friend and ally to Monet and Sisley, who both struggled, as indeed Pissarro did, long and hard to secure their place in the art world.

Although Pissarro was able to instil confidence in others, he was himself deeply uneasy about his own ability and only settled into a mode of expression which began to satisfy him very late in his life, following a brief but productive flirtation with Neo-Impressionism.

PISSARRO
Self-portrait
1873
ABOVE

PISSARRO
Sunset at Eragny
oil on canvas
1896.
54.5 × 65cm
(22 × 26in)
OPPOSITE

LIFE AND WORKS: CAMILLE PISSARRO (1830–1903)

Remember that I have the temperament of a peasant, I am melancholy, harsh and savage in my works. It is only in the long run that I can expect to please, and then only those who have a grain of indulgence.

CAMILLE PISSARRO

Camille Jacob Pissarro, "the First Impressionist" as Cézanne referred to him, was born on 10th July 1830 on the island of St Thomas in the Danish West Indies (now the U.S. Virgin Islands), the fourth son of Abraham Pissarro, a French Jew from Bordeaux, and Rachel Manzana-Pommié, a Creole from Dominica who had been widowed and was seven years older than her second husband. Abraham Pissarro ran a general store in Charlotte Amalie, the capital and port of St Thomas.

Though he and his family lived on a tiny island thousands of miles from France, Abraham Pissarro was keen to bring up his children in the French manner, so between the ages of twelve and seventeen Camille attended a boarding school, the Académie Savary in Passy, a suburb of Paris. M. Savary, the director of the Académie, is said to have encouraged the boy's artistic leanings by imploring him to draw coconut palms from nature when he returned to the West Indies. In 1847 Camille was back in St Thomas working in his father's store and he must have indeed followed M. Savary's advice in his spare time, for nine years later (in Paris again) he was painting tropical landscapes from memory.

Camille remained with his family in St Thomas until 1853 when, after five years of working as a clerk, its charms were no longer able to detain him. He decided he had to see more of the world and took off without parental consent to Venezuela with the Danish artist, Fritz Melbye. For the next two years they rented a studio in Caracas where Pissarro practised drawing and attempted his first watercolours under the thoughtful eye of Melbye who had studied at the Copenhagen Academy and was able to teach his friend the basics of the Academic Style. By the time he had obtained his father's blessing and sailed to Paris to study with Melbye's brother Anton, Pissarro was already an accomplished landscape painter.

The Exposition Universelle of 1855 was in its last few days when Pissarro arrived in Paris. Courbet's Realist Pavilion was creating a stir, but Pissarro was more interested in the few landscapes by Corot on show and later introduced himself to the master landscapist. During the next couple of years Pissarro worked as Anton Melbye's assistant, took some private lessons at the Ecole and studied at the free Académie Suisse where he met Claude Monet; he was also an occasional pupil of Corot, describing himself as such in his first submission to the Salon in 1859.

Pissarro passed the Salon hurdle at the first attempt. His parents had recently returned to France and settled in Paris, and were suitably impressed (and no doubt relieved) that their youngest son had begun to make his mark in the art world. The Salon was the summit of exhibitions and Pissarro's carefully worked landscape of Montmorency had enough of Corot in it to succeed in academic terms, but it also proved that Pissarro's talent was to be uncompromising. The move from the exotic Virgin Islands and South America to what the art historian Linda Nochlin calls "the infinitely civilized" French countryside had produced in Pissarro a lighter, more naturalistic vision than that of Corot. In the years to come he was frequently to be accused of painting vulgar and unaesthetic landscapes far from Corot's comparatively idealized works.

From his earliest drawings in St Thomas to his death in 1903, Pissarro's style and method were in a continual state of flux. As the art historian John House has said, "to chart Pissarro's stylistic evolution . . . we meet in turn Corot, Daubigny, Courbet, Jongkind, Monet, Cézanne, Renoir, Millet, Seurat, Turner, and Monet again." Although he was the oldest of the Impressionists, Pissarro never ceased assimilating the work of others in an artistic evolution

COROT
Dardagny, Morning
oil on canvas
c.1853. 26 × 47cm
(10 × 19in)
Pissarro had seen the few Corots on show at the 1855 Exposition Universelle and a year later went to see the master landscapist. Corot's style was a profound influence on Pissarro for many years. This small, sketchy picture displays the freer side of Corot which suited Pissarro's early vision.

which is unparalleled among his contemporaries. In the late 1850s and early 1860s the Salon and the French art world were in a deep debate about the acceptability of Daubigny's sketchy *plein-airisme* and the consequences of Courbet's realism. Having succeeded on the safer ground of Corot, Pissarro began to appreciate the attempts of Daubigny and Courbet to paint what they saw and wanted to see. At the age of twenty-nine Pissarro met Monet, ten years his junior, at the Académie Suisse and soon became part of a new generation of artists fired by the example of Courbet and Daubigny, impatient with the academic landscape.

Unlike Monet, Renoir, Sisley, and the other budding Impressionists with whom he was soon to have a remarkable relationship, Pissarro's view of the world had already become deeply politicized. The glory of the Second Empire was skin deep as far as he

could see and the dehumanizing effects of rapid industrialization hidden behind the glittering façade of the Empire were not lost on him. He grew increasingly attracted to the extreme radicalism of Proudhon and Prince Kropotkin. Proudhon had said that "art should show us exactly as we are, not in a mediated fantasy that no longer represents us." The artist he had in mind for his project was Courbet; Pissarro was already well acquainted with Courbet's work in the late 1850s and had read Proudhon's huge tract *On Justice in the Revolution and the Church*, published in 1858. Somewhat anarchic by nature, Pissarro began to espouse some of Proudhon's anarcho-federalist ideals and was to become more avowedly anarchist as the years went by. (Proudhon was, as the art historian Ralph Shikes points out, "a passionate advocate of Justice, Liberty, and Equality, yet his Equality did not embrace universal suffrage; blacks, whom he regarded as inferior; and women, equally inferior, whose place he felt was in the home.") The task of the artist, as Pissarro was to say many years later, echoing Proudhon, "is to seek with our own senses the elements of what surrounds us. This can only be achieved by observing nature with our own contemporary sensibility. It is a serious mistake to believe that every form of art is not closely linked to its time."

In 1860 when it seemed little could shake the foundations of the Second Empire, Proudhon's views were considered dangerous but tolerated. Despite his growing convictions, Pissarro's talents clearly

MILLET
The Gleaners
oil on canvas
1857. 83.5 × 111cm
(33 × 44in)
Millet was also an important early influence on Pissarro, who was attracted to subjects like this and continued to paint them throughout his career. Millet's plain and sentimental paeans to peasant life were criticized for the "vulgarity" of their subject matter, but formed an important model for artists such as Pissarro and later van Gogh.

lay in the reality of nature and agriculture, in landscapes with figures – what one critic has called humanist landscape – not social realism, although the two could combine successfully to a certain extent in his *Railway Bridge at Pontoise* (*Le Pont de chemin de fer à Pontoise*) of 1860, and yet prove stilted and sentimental in

Donkey Ride at La Roche-Guyan (*Promenade à l'âne à La Roche-Guyon*), what Shikes calls "the only canvas of his career with an overt social message."

Several important relationships developed for Pissarro in 1860. Working in the countryside around Paris one of his constant companions was Ludovic Piette, a

PISSARRO
Woman Reading
oil on canvas
1860. 26.5 × 29cm
(10 × 11in)
The sitter is Julie Vellay, the maid of Pissarro's mother, whom he met the same year, and who was quite a few years younger than him. They had seven children and married ten years later, in 1870, while they were in London.

PISSARRO
Banks of the Marne in Winter
oil on canvas
1866. 92 × 150cm (36 × 59in)
The influence of Corot is manifest in this bare work, which was shown at the Salon, where the subject was found vulgar and the painting ugly. It was indeed not decorative enough for its time, but Pissarro was never concerned by prettiness.

landscape painter four years older than Pissarro who had studied at the famous atelier of Couture and then at the Académie Suisse. Pissarro struck up a life-long friendship with Piette, who was moderately well off and had a farm at Montfoucault in Brittany which in future years became indispensable to the penniless Pissarro. At about this time Pissarro became closely attached to Julie Vellay, the daughter of a viticulturist from Burgundy, who had found employment as his mother's maid. There had been no Salon in 1860, but after his initial success two years earlier the vagaries of the Salon were against Pissarro this time. The jury was severe and rejected his entry but accepted Manet's *Guitar Player* (*Le Joueur de guitare*) with an honourable mention. Pissarro continued to work in Paris, copying

at the Louvre and working at the Académie Suisse where he met two important allies, Paul Cézanne, on whom he was to have a great influence, and Armand Guillaumin.

1863 was the year of the Salon des Refusés and the scandal of Manet's *Luncheon on the Grass* (*Déjeuner sur l'herbe*) which over-shadowed the contributions of Pissarro, Cézanne, Jongkind, and Guillaumin and launched the reluctant Manet as a figurehead of the avant-garde. The year had begun auspiciously for Pissarro and Julie Vellay; in February the first of their seven children, Lucien, was born (Julie had in fact suffered a miscarriage the year before). Pissarro was a devoted father to his children; his extensive correspondence with Lucien, who moved to London in the 1890s to set up a book illustration press, forms a large part of our knowledge about Pissarro's later life.

Two years later Abraham Pissarro died, precipitating a financial crisis for Camille Pissarro and his growing family – they now had a daughter, Jeanne. The Salon of 1864 had accepted two landscapes from the artist, described in the catalogue as a pupil of Corot and (Anton) Melbye, and Pissarro appeared in the Salon until rejected along with Renoir, Sisley, and Monet in 1867.

Despite this relatively steady success rate at the most important of art markets, Pissarro's sales were few and far between; he was already beginning to call upon the largesse of friends such as Ludovic Piette whose farmhouse in Montfoucault he had visited in 1864. At this time he also began to fall out with Corot who did not approve of the increasing influence of Courbet in Pissarro's work and thereafter Pissarro stopped calling himself a pupil of Corot. The painting Pissarro showed at the 1866 Salon, *Banks of the Marne in Winter* (*Les Rives de la Marne en hiver*) drew the praise of Zola for its modernity, whilst another critic said: "M. Pissarro is not commonplace for want of the ability to be picturesque, he has used his robust and exuberant talent to depict the

vulgarity of the modern world." The influence of Corot's subdued pigments, as well as Courbet's palette knife technique is evident here, but even at this early stage in his development Pissarro's choice and control of his admittedly banal subject stands out as an intensely personal vision of the countryside (near Pissarro's home at the time, La Varenne-Saint-Hilaire) that he painted.

By 1867 Pissarro and his family had moved to Pontoise, a village on the river Oise near Auvers, where

PISSARRO
Springtime in Louveciennes
oil on canvas
c.1868–69. 53 × 82cm
(21 × 32in)
The Pissarros had recently moved to Louveciennes, a small town on the banks of the Seine not far from Marly, where Sisley lived, and Bougival, where Monet worked. This landscape is still close in style to Corot, especially in the rendering of the trees on the right.

they remained until 1869 and then settled in Louveciennes. Pissarro worked consistently outdoors at landscapes during these years but kept a studio in Paris and was close to the rapidly growing movement that met in the Café Guerbois. The 1867 Salon which coincided with the Exposition Universelle was particularly conservative in its selections and Pissarro, one of the many *refusés*, had joined Renoir, Sisley, Monet, Bazille, and Cézanne in signing a petition demanding another Salon des Refusés. There was now talk of an independent exhibition amongst the Gleyre students and Pissarro, Cézanne, and Degas. Pissarro was by now deeply involved in the emerging group and was to play an increasing role in its future development. Daubigny's inclusion on the Salon's jury the next year secured the exhibition of two of Pissarro's Pontoise landscapes, moving Zola to pronounce Pissarro "one of the three or four true painters of our day. I have rarely encountered a technique that is so sure . . . *C'est là la campagne moderne* [this is truly the modern countryside]." Sadly this praise was of little avail to the Pissarro family, now in financial straits. Their income was so erratic that Camille was occasionally forced to join with Armand Guillaumin decorating shop fronts and blinds.

A brief period of relative calm and consolidation ensued in Louveciennes, where Pissarro's researches into landscape continued. He was joined by Claude Monet, who had been working with Renoir at La Grenouillère (Pissarro had briefly worked there as well during the summer). In the winter of 1869–70 under varying weather conditions both artists painted similar views of the road to Versailles where Pissarro's house stood.

The outbreak of war on 19th July 1870 forced the Pissarro family to move to safety, first to Piette's farm in Brittany and then in December they crossed the English Channel to a suburb of London where Pissarro's mother was already living. There he finally married Julie Vellay, already pregnant with their third child.

Monet had fled to London as well, and through the auspices of the sympathetic dealer Durand-Ruel, also a refugee in London, Pissarro made contact with him: "Monet and I were very enthusiastic over the London land-scapes," recalled Pissarro in a letter of 1902. "Monet worked in the parks whilst I, living in Lower Norwood, at that time a charming suburb, studied the effect of fog, snow, and springtime. We worked from nature . . . We also visited the museums. The watercolours and

PISSARRO
The Diligence at Louveciennes
oil on canvas
1870. 25.5 × 35.7cm
(10 × 14in)

Pissarro has at last found his own style: the brushstrokes are less unified and he captures well the atmosphere of a rainy day. The diligence was the public coach transporting local passengers, here seen on its slow round.

paintings of Constable and Turner and the canvases of Old Crome [i.e. John Crome, 1768–1821, leading artist of the Norwich School of landscapists] have certainly had an influence upon us. We admired Gainsborough, Lawrence, Reynolds, etc., but were struck chiefly by the landscape painters who shared more in our aim with regard to *plein-air*, light and fugitive effects." As the art historian Phoebe Pool notes, Pissarro's initial delight at the English landscapists was grudgingly tempered. In the last year of his life he wrote to Lucien saying, "Turner and Constable . . . showed us in their work that they had no understanding of the analysis of shadow, which in Turner's painting is simply used as an effect, a mere absence of light. As far as tone division is concerned, Turner proved its value although he did not apply it correctly and naturally."

The important contact with Durand-Ruel aside, Pissarro's fortunes did not improve in London; the public were not keen to buy his paintings and the Royal Academy's annual exhibition refused both his and Monet's work. Twelve paintings and some studies survive from Pissarro's time in London, ranging from the highly impressionistic *Fox Hill, Upper Norwood* and *Dulwich College* to the more highly polished *The Avenue, Sydenham,* which Durand-Ruel eventually bought in 1871, but which Pissarro must have hoped to sell to the London market.

The net result in artistic terms of Pissarro's exile in London, his contact with Monet and the

PISSARRO
Dulwich College
oil on canvas
c.1870. 50 × 61cm
(20 × 24in)
Save the rather systematic rendering of the branches, the careful if plain rendering of some of Corot's work has now disappeared from Pissarro's. Dulwich College was and remains one of the landmarks of the area.

CÉZANNE
Dr Gachet's House at Auvers
oil on canvas
1873. 46 × 38cm (18 × 15in)
ABOVE Cézanne worked with Pissarro between 1872 and 1874, and his technique improved considerably under Pissarro's tuition. Here we can see how Cézanne emulates Pissarro's style, abandoning a thick impasto worked with a palette knife for a lighter and more sober rendering.

PISSARRO
Self-portrait
oil on canvas
1873. 56 × 46.5cm
(22 × 18in)
OPPOSITE Pissarro was only forty-three when this portrait was made, but he looks much older by our standards. Renoir complained of being old at the same age.

English landscape school, was a freer handling of brighter pigments, using the swiftly applied patches of colour which Monet had been developing since La Grenouillère and was now employing to great effect in his views of the Thames. Compared to Monet, now approaching Impressionism *par excellence*, Pissarro's onging debt to the first of his mentors, Corot, as well as to Daubigny and Courbet is still evident in *The Avenue, Sydenham*. Solidity and consonance of composition characterize his work in comparison to Monet's search for "fugitive effects" in light and water.

The fall of the Paris Commune and the end of war in 1871 allowed Pissarro and his family to return to Louveciennes. What they saw when they got there horrified them. The Prussians had commandeered their house and used it as a butchery. Of the 1,500 paintings the artist had stored there, only about forty remained; the rest had been ripped from their stretchers and placed on the ground for the soldiers to walk on. Pissarro found the abused canvases discarded on the compost heap. Undeterred, Pissarro carried on painting as prodigiously as before. In November their second son, Georges, was born. In 1872 they moved back to Pontoise where they remained until 1882. Cézanne, invited by Pissarro to continue his landscape studies in Pontoise, arrived in the winter of 1872 with his companion Hortense Fiquet and their son Paul. They took up residence in a local hotel, later moving to nearby Auvers-sur-Oise. Cézanne's *House of the Hanged Man*

PISSARRO
Red Roofs
oil on canvas 1877.
54.5 × 65.5cm (22 × 26in)
*ABOVE Pissarro painted Red Roofs
during the winter of 1876–77. It was a
cluster of houses at the bottom of the Côtes
des Boeufs, very near Pissarro's house.*

PISSARRO
La Côte des Boeufs at the
Hermitage, near Pontoise
oil on canvas 1877. 115 × 87.5cm
(45 × 34in) *OPPOSITE This year
Cézanne had returned from the south of
France to work with Pissarro. Here we
find a similar view of cottages seen
through trees, and a hill blocking part of
the background. Pissarro was beginning
to apply thicker coats of paint, giving
more texture to his canvases.*

at Auvers *(La Maison du pendu à
Auvers)* from this period is greatly
influenced by Pissarro's increasingly
impressionistic style.

Pissarro's fortunes were temporarily looking up. Auctions in
Paris were fetching high prices,
whilst the influential, sympathetic
and extremely wealthy journalist
and art critic Théodore Duret, the
Comte de Brie, was beginning to
champion the work of Pissarro and
others in the group. The soon-to-
be-named Impressionists, including
Pissarro, were thrashing out the
details of the new *Société anonyme*
that they were about to form
in order to launch their first
exhibition. Pissarro was deeply

involved in organizing the new
venture, foreseeing a sort of
co-operative or collective bizarrely
based on the principles of the
Pontoise bakers' union and the
*Association des artistes, peintres
d'histoire et de genre, etc* which he
had joined thirteen years before.
Renoir, Monet and the rest of the
group found the complexities of
Pissarro's plan too much and
eventually a joint stock company
was founded with the fifteen artists
as equal shareholders. Further
tension was created by Pissarro
insisting on Cézanne and
Guillaumin joining the *Société's*
exhibition but Pissarro had his way.
Duret was against the whole idea of

PISSARRO
The Garden at the Hermitage
oil on canvas
1877. 55 × 46cm (22 × 18in)
ABOVE Abandoning for once the open country, Pissarro depicts two of his children in the family garden, which does not look as well cared for as Monet's.

PISSARRO
The Seamstress
pastel on canvas
1881. 25 × 20cm (10 × 8in)
OPPOSITE In this small study, Pissarro depicts the humble life of a peasant woman in the peace of her home.

an independent exhibition and urged Pissarro to follow Manet's example and stick to the Salon. This Pissarro ignored and thus remained faithful to the concept of the Impressionist exhibitions; he went on to contribute to all eight.

April 1874 proved to be an eventful, albeit traumatic month for Pissarro. In the Impressionists' first exhibition Pissarro's innovative landscapes were condemned along with the others. When the exhibition closed Pissarro was forced to appeal to Piette for help. Following his critical failure, Pissarro's nine-year-old daughter Jeanne died the same month.

Pissarro was now almost forty-five years old. Fifteen years later in 1890 he wrote a letter to his niece, Esther Isaacson, summing up his career thus far: "I began to understand my feelings and know what I wanted in my forties – but only vaguely; at the age of fifty, in 1880, I conceived an idea of [artistic] unity without being able to render it; at sixty I am now beginning to see the possibility of rendering it." Pissarro's career was indeed a long and arduous search for the perfect method of expressing himself and his ideas. Until his sixty-second year when Durand-Ruel mounted a hugely successful retrospective of his work he was permanently in dire straits as his family continued to grow. Yet despite these pressures, he never begrudged anyone advice and encouragement. Younger painters, beginning with Cézanne in 1872, Gauguin in 1877, and later Matisse and Picabia sought him out. Cézanne revered him, saying he was like a father to him, "*un peu comme le bon Dieu*" ("a little like the good Lord"). Mary Cassatt thought he was such a good teacher he could have taught the stones to draw.

By the time of the last Impressionist exhibition in 1886 the great teacher was himself in an artistic crisis. The intervening years had seen him contribute to every Impressionist show and often cajole the other members of the group into accepting the works of younger artists such as Gauguin. He had been helped along by commissions from the successful patissier Eugène Murer, who had also bought a hotel room for him in Rouen where he spent considerable periods painting the cityscape. A printing partnership with Degas and Mary Cassatt had been successful, Durand-Ruel had supported him when and as he could, and so he had managed to get by. In 1884 the Pissarro family had moved to Eragny where they eventually bought the house they had leased (with the aid of a loan from Monet which Pissarro scrupulously repaid). Meanwhile Pissarro's interest in the human figure, especially the peasant women who were so much a part of the landscape, had come to dominate his work as a fundamental expression of his humanism. As Ralph Shikes observes:

Often he paints the grubby kitchen gardens, quite understandably paintings of little appeal to a self-conscious middle class. His agricultural workers – members of the peasant family or day labourers – carry buckets of water, herd the cows, feed the chickens. They are mostly women performing lowly

chores. They are not heroic figures but simple humanity observed in the cadenced rhythm of the seasons . . . as they perform their [daily] tasks.

But the method of expressing all this had become problematic. The web of comma like brush-strokes which had now become his trademark seemed to have reached its logical conclusion and he was casting about for new ways of painting. A harder edge was called for. Impressionism seemed to have had its day; Renoir for example had recently found himself in a similar stylistic dead-end and was developing an overtly linear, Neo-Classical style; years before, Cézanne had abandoned a softer vision of the world and was absorbed in lines, volumes, and planes. In October 1885 Pissarro met the young Georges Seurat who was developing a new technique, Divisionism, based on several theories going back to Chevreul. Pissarro too had read the new colour theories proposed by the American colour theorists Charles Henry and Ogden Rood, and with Paul Signac he found common cause in Seurat's juxtaposition of small dots of pure pigment to create the forms of a painting. "I am totally convinced of the progressive nature of this art," he wrote to Lucien, "and certain that in time it will yield extraordinary results. I do not accept the snobbish judgments of romantic Impressionists in whose interest it is to fight against new tendencies. I accept the challenge, that's all."

At the age of fifty-five Pissarro became a Neo-Impressionist; his

PISSARRO
Harvesting Hay
oil on canvas
c. 1887. 51 × 66cm (20 × 26in)
While retaining his familiar subject matter, which Seurat had also treated in small studies, Pissarro is now adapting Pointillism to his own style, and the woman in the middle has lost the soft and natural posture of his earlier figures.

PISSARRO
Landscape at Eragny
oil on canvas
1895. 60 × 73.5cm
(24 × 29in)
*Another example of Pissarro's late
Pointillism. This is an afterthought –
he had renounced the technique a
few years earlier, and it has none
of the dogmatic coldness seen in
Seurat's works.*

anarchism had also become more
fervent. Writing later to Lucien, he
said: "I firmly believe that our
anarchist philosophy is linked to
our work and therefore disagreeable
to current thought." Signac and
Seurat were also sympathetic to the
aims of anarchism, although it is
difficult to see any concrete link
between these amorphous aims and
their work. In any case Pissarro's
Neo-Impressionism was to last
barely five years, and was resisted on
the one hand by Durand-Ruel
who refused to buy his Divisionist
works and on the other by
Impressionists who were loath to

exhibit in the company of
Divisionists. Nevertheless Pissarro
secured what amounted to a
separate Divisionist Room in the
final Impressionist exhibition of
1886, where he, his son Lucien,
Signac, and Seurat showed work
which attracted both acclaim
and horror.

The tedious physical process of
painting in what was variously
called the Neo-Impressionist,
Pointillist, or Divisionist technique
of dots took its toll on Pissarro and
reduced the number of canvases
(normally high) which he could
finish. In May 1889 his mother died

at the age of ninety-four. The same year Pissarro began to suffer from an eye infection, forcing him to work indoors, but not inhibiting his flow of work. He abandoned the limitations of Divisionism the next year and began a phase of painting urban and quayside landscapes in Paris, Rouen, Le Hâvre, and Dieppe, as well as in London. The years between 1889 and 1900 were perhaps the most productive of his life; in 1896 he was earning

sufficient sums to begin paying back the money he had borrowed from Monet. Truly anarchic to the end, Pissarro became more committed to the cause as he approached his seventies. Back in the days of the Café Guerbois he had once suggested burning down the Louvre; now, in 1894, his anarchist sympathies forced him to spend four months in Knocke, Belgium after the knifing to death of Président Sadi Carnot by an

PISSARRO
Paris, Place du Hâvre
oil on canvas
1893. 60 × 73cm (24 × 29in)
Dissatisfied with Pointillism, Pissarro looked instead for a different kind of subject, and produced many cityscapes in his later years, most of them seen from the window of rooms high up above Paris, Rouen and Dieppe.

Italian anarchist. During the Dreyfus Affair, which practically tore *fin de siècle* France apart, he came out staunchly on Zola's side and against the entrenched anti-Semitism of the French military which had clumsily framed an innocent Jewish captain-of-the-guard and led to his exile and imprisonment.

Camille Pissarro died in Paris on 13th November 1903 of blood poisoning caused by an abscess of the prostate: his homeopathic doctor had attempted to cure it without an operation. His last years were marked by international honour and public acclaim. Of all the Impressionists he was perhaps the best loved and respected by his friends, fellow artists and protégés. After Pissarro's death Gauguin said of him, despite the severe criticism he had received from Pissarro: *"Ce fut un de mes maîtres. Je ne le renie pas."* ("He was one of my masters. I cannot renounce him.")

PISSARRO
Boulevard Montmarte, Paris
oil on canvas
1897. 72 × 91cm
(28 × 36in)
ABOVE Renoir was very critical of Pissarro's cityscapes. He might more justly have said that compared to Monet, Pissarro's style had not evolved as much. There is indeed no marked difference between some of Monet's cityscapes of 1876 and this painting, made twenty years later.

PISSARRO
Boulevard Montmarte by Night
oil on canvas
1897. 53.5 × 65cm (21 × 26in)
RIGHT Both pictures were painted from the Hôtel de Russie at the corner of the boulevard des Italiens and the rue Drouot in Paris, in an area familiar to the Impressionist group. The night view presented a challenge which seems to have stimulated the artist, and Pissarro met it with great success, in a decidedly impressionistic way, giving life to the flicker of street lights and to the reflections in the rain on the pavement.

E DOUARD MANET was the figurehead of a generation of artists who saw him as a champion of experimental and non-conformist art. As a conventional member of the bourgeoisie who desired nothing better than to be acclaimed by society at the Salon, Manet's career was marked by misunderstanding from both sides. As a friend of Baudelaire, he was at the very forefront of the artistic avant-garde, yet he remained personally conservative and eager to please. It was his ability to create something new from the most conventional of subjects that ensured his continuing fame as well as a deeply felt ambivalence amongst his critics, who until recently have expressed contradictory views that he was both a genius and lacking in imagination. His achievements lay in the ambiguity and unrivalled originality with which he portrayed the Paris of his day, as epitomized in the *Bar at the Folies-Bergère* and the *Corner in a Café-concert* – two paintings which more than any of his contemporaries' encapsulated impressions of an age of decaying and transitory brilliance.

FANTIN-LATOUR
Edouard Manet
1867.
ABOVE

MANET
The Walk
oil on canvas
c.1880.
92.5 × 70.5cm
(36 × 28in)
OPPOSITE

MANET
Copy of Tintoretto's Self-portrait
oil on canvas
1854. 61 × 50cm (24 × 20in)
ABOVE This is one of the numerous old masters copied by Manet. He was a registered copyist at the Louvre but also worked in the Rijksmuseum of Amsterdam, and in Florence, Rome and Venice. Manet was a vital pivot in a long tradition which he sincerely acknowledged.

LIFE AND WORKS: EDOUARD MANET (1832–1883)

. . . a revolutionary painter who loved society and had always dreamt of the success only Paris can offer – the flattery of the ladies, the warm embrace of their salons, a life of luxury hurtling through admiring crowds.

EMILE ZOLA

Edouard Manet was born in Paris on 23rd January 1832, the oldest son of Auguste Manet, Head of Personnel at the French Ministry of Justice, and Eugénie Désirée Fournier, a diplomat's daughter.

Manet could have become a successful lawyer, which is what his father had in mind for him, but it was perhaps the influence of his artistic mother Eugénie and his uncle Edmond Fournier, a great connoisseur of art, that quashed the idea early on. From the age of fifteen Manet and his friend at the exclusive Collège Rollin, Antonin Proust, received special drawing lessons and were taken on instructive tours of the Paris museums by Edmond Fournier. At sixteen Manet rebelled against his father's wish to enter him in the Faculty of Law, declared his desire to be an artist, forced a compromise with his father (it was more of a ruse than anything) and joined the Navy. He failed the Naval entrance examinations but set sail nonetheless on 9th December 1848 at the age of sixteen as an officer cadet on the ship *Le Hâvre et Guadeloupe* bound for Rio de Janeiro.

On his return to France the next year Manet failed the Naval examinations once again and finally swayed his father to his artistic ambitions. The baggage Manet brought back from the Americas was crammed with drawings to prove his vocation.

In the Paris of the 1850s there were several independent ateliers where a budding artist could study, and Manet chose one of the most celebrated, that of Thomas Couture in the rue de Laval (now the rue Victor-Massé). Couture had beguiled the Salon of 1847 with his epic painting *The Romans of the Decadence* and was famous both as a painter and as a liberal teacher. Manet remained at Couture's from 1850 to 1856, studying the master's teaching, copying (amongst other things a Velazquez) at the Louvre and occasionally causing trouble in the atelier, as Antonin Proust remembered: "On Mondays, the day when a pose was to be struck for the rest of the week, Manet would invariably fight with Couture's models . . . Mounting the podium they would assume their traditional and exaggerated poses. 'Are you incapable of being natural?' Manet would cry, 'Is that how you stand when you're buying a bundle of radish at the green grocer's?'" Proust described another incident which sheds some light on Manet's developing wit and his relationship with Couture: "One day Manet had managed to make Gilbert (a model) assume a natural pose, half dressed. Couture walked into the atelier and threw a fit in front of the clothed model. 'So you pay Gilbert to *keep his clothes on?* Who is responsible for this stupidity?' 'I am,' said Manet. 'Come now, my poor boy,' said Couture, 'you will never be anything but the Daumier of your time.' Later Manet is supposed to have told Antonin, "The Daumier of my time! At least that would be better than being the Coypel of it." (Coypel was not a fashionable painter at that time.)

Despite these frivolities Manet was greatly indebted to Couture, an opponent of the all-pervading academic style and its constrictions. Couture's advice to his students was: "Make sure first of all that you have mastered material procedures; then think of nothing and produce with a fresh mind and hearty spirit whatever you feel like doing." This was exactly what Manet was to do, building on a complete mastery of technique and a deep appreciation of the old masters in order to make his revolutionary (or evolutionary) mark. A foretaste of what was to come is supplied by Antonin Proust, who remembered Manet drawing a picture in 1851 which showed the identification of bodies in the Montmartre cemetery, victims of the December *coup d'état* by Louis Napoleon. Manet was already a fierce republican; he had written to his father from Rio de Janeiro: "Try to keep a good republic for us against our return; I'm afraid Louis Napoleon is not a very good republican." How right he was; the corpses in Montmartre

MANET
The Parents of the Artist
oil on canvas
1860. 110 × 90cm (43 × 35in)
OPPOSITE BOTTOM The austere M. Manet does not indeed look like the sort of father a son could confide in about his illegitimate offspring. Manet never told his father about Léon, born to his twenty-year-old piano teacher Suzanne Leenhoff, and married only after his father's death.

MANET
The Absinthe Drinker
oil on canvas
1859. 177.5 × 103cm
(70 × 41in)
ABOVE Absinthe had far too bad a reputation to be an acceptable subject for the Salon. Manet found his low-life models in the Batignolles area where he lived. The model here is the ragpicker Colardet.

MANET
Young Woman in Spanish Costume
(*DETAIL*)
oil on canvas
1862. 95 × 113cm (37 × 45in)
*RIGHT The pose is that of Goya's
Maja. Whereas Goya painted
both a nude and a dressed-up
version, Manet chose to dress
her as a torero.*

MANET
The Spanish Dancers
oil on canvas
1862. 61 × 91cm (24 × 36in)
*BELOW All things Spanish
appealed to the French Romantics
in ascendence during Manet's
youth. Manet could not resist the
opportunity of painting members
of a ballet company that was
touring Paris in 1862. The
group in this picture includes
Lola de Valence.*

proved that Manet's fears for the Second Republic were well founded – it had lasted barely two years after his return from South America.

In January 1852 a son, Léon, was born to Suzanne Leenhoff, Manet's twenty-year-old piano teacher with whom he had been having an affair since 1850. Eugénie Manet knew of the illegitimate birth, but she and Manet conspired to keep this from the austere and conservative Auguste Manet, passing the child off as Suzanne's brother and Manet's godson, even after Suzanne and Manet's marriage. Manet's strict adherence to form held sway, as it would in other matters, and Suzanne, like so many other mistresses, companions, and courtesans, was set up in an apartment to keep her out of harm's way until it was safe for her to emerge into society.

Manet left Couture's atelier around Easter 1856 and moved into a studio in the rue Lavoisier with another painter, Albert de Balleroy. He then made a tour of Holland, Germany, Austria, and Italy ending in Venice, visiting museums and studying the old masters. In 1859 Manet made his first submission, *The Absinthe Drinker* (*L'Absinthe*) to the Salon. It was summarily rejected on several counts, notably those of immorality and vulgarity; only Delacroix voted for it. The next year Manet made the acquain-tance of the poet and art critic Charles Baudelaire, eleven years his senior, who had published his masterpiece, a collection of poems called *Les Fleurs du mal* (*The Flowers of Evil*) in 1857. The poems had caused outrage and several were banned. Flaubert's *Madame Bovary* had suffered a similar fate in 1856. The early years of Louis Napoleon's reign were difficult ones for literature and the avant-garde, of which Manet was rapidly becoming an important if somewhat reluctant member. He was now moving in two social milieux; upper middle-class salon society and the Bohemian demimonde of

MANET
The Old Musician
oil on canvas
1862. 187.5 × 248.5cm (74 × 98in)
This painting is a very large composition which retains a stillness typical of many of Manet's works. Again, he found his models near his home: he re-used the figure of The Absinthe Drinker, *who stands on the right, wearing a top hat. The old man was the gypsy Jean Lagrène. The cut-off figure along the right edge of the picture represents the Wandering Jew. All these people are poor, but Manet did not attempt to depict them in a romantic or sentimental manner. Rather, he displays a detachment from his subject matter that was later to bring accusations of coldness and impersonality.*

MANET
Battle of the Kearsarge and
the Alabama
oil on canvas
c.1865. 139 × 130cm
(55 × 51in)
*ABOVE Always interested in current
events and no doubt recalling his own
days at sea before he became a painter,
Manet painted two scenes of this
remarkable episode in the American
Civil War, which took place off the
coast of Boulogne. In the second
picture, the* Kearsarge *is seen
damaged and moored along the jetty.*

MANET
The Execution of the Emperor
Maximilian
oil on canvas
1867. 195 × 259cm (77 × 102in)
*RIGHT In this advanced study, the
firing squad is wearing Mexican
outfits and the faces of the victims
are featureless. The news of the
execution had just reached Paris,
and to Manet the incident illustrated
all too well the bankruptcy of
Napoleon III's regime.*

Baudelaire and his friends where revolutionary new ideas were inspired and thrashed out. Baudelaire, with whom Manet became very close, died in agony of the effects of aphasia and syphilis in 1867. His anguished romanticism can be heard in these lines from *Les Fleurs du mal*:

> – *Ô douleur! ô douleur! Le Temps*
> *mange la vie,*
> *Et l'obscur Ennemi qui nous*
> *ronge le coeur*
> *Du sang que nous perdons*
> *croît et se fortifie!*

> – O agony, agony! Time eats
> away at life,
> And the obscure Foe which
> gnaws on our hearts
> Grows ever stronger on the
> blood we lose!

Manet's close friendship with Baudelaire inspired his art in other ways, however. It is noticeable that after *The Absinthe Drinker*, and Manet's encounter with the extraordinarily decadent Baudelaire, the artist avoided further images of rank dissolution. The less decadent side of Baudelaire, his penetrating art criticism and demand for an urban "painter of modern life", was of more interest, in fact, to Manet than the last torments of a dying genius.

Manet's early interest in politics did not abate and he remained keenly aware of current events throughout his life. In June 1864 he went to the port of Cherbourg to witness a bizarre incident of the American Civil War playing itself out. A corvette of the Union Navy, the *Kearsarge*, was attacking and pursuing a Confederate privateer, the *Alabama*, which had been detained in the French docks.

Manet painted a gripping picture of the scene. Three years later he painted the first version of *The Execution of the Emperor Maximilian*. The painting was banned as being too sensitive a political subject for exhibition at Manet's pavilion in the place d'Alma during the 1867 Exposition Universelle. Indeed, from the scandal of *Luncheon on the Grass* at the Salon des Refusés of 1863 onwards Manet was constantly (and it must be said unwillingly) at odds with the authorities, both artistic and political. Manet's subject matter was at the forefront of modernity and strained the limits of the acceptable. He had side-stepped the social realism of Proudhon and Courbet and worked initially under the aesthetic veil of *l'art pour l'art* (Art for Art's Sake), as exemplified in its most frivolous literary form by these two stanzas from a poem by Théophile Gautier:

> *Que tu me plais dans cette robe*
> *Qui te déshabille si bien,*

> *Faisant jaillir ta gorge en globe,*
> *Montrant tout nu ton bras païen!*
> *Frêle comme une aile d'abeille,*
> *Frais comme un coeur de rose-thé*
> *Son tissu, caresse vermeille,*
> *Voltige autour de ta beauté.*

> How you please me in this dress
> Which undresses you so well,
> Letting your breast burst forth,
> Showing quite nude your
>   pagan arm!
> Fragile as a bee's wing,
> Fresh as the heart of a tea-rose,
> Its tissue, a vermillion caress,
> Flutters about your beautiousness.

> *A une robe rose*
> (*To a Pink Dress*)
> FROM *EMAUX ET CAMÉES*,
> 1852

Apart from its concision – brevity was becoming Manet's own stylistic watchword – and its eroticism, *A une robe rose* also gives us a taste of just how small the Bohemian world of Paris was; the poem is dedicated to Apollonie Sabatier, delectable courtesane, and the *Présidente* of the infamous Club des Hashishins frequented by Baudelaire and Gautier, an object herself of extreme (and unrequited) passion from Baudelaire who immortalized her in a cycle of poems within *Les Fleurs du mal*. (She was also given permanent fame in other ways; the sculptor Clésinger made a cast of her body and then modelled it in marble to the delight of the 1847 Salon.)

The influence of Baudelaire's ideas in the early part of Manet's career can be seen in his painting, *Music in the Tuileries Gardens*, which answers the call for a painting of modern life by doing just that;

MANET
Olympia watercolour study
1863.
Manet undertook several studies for the scandalous painting.

depicting the bourgeoisie outdoors on a summer's day together with a smattering of Bohemians. Baudelaire and Gautier are among the strollers.

By 1865 *Olympia* had turned the art world upside down, and Manet was the focus of the younger artists' admiration. In that year he began to frequent the Café Guerbois, where contemporary accounts testify to Manet's *sang-froid* and incisive wit in the midst of his colleagues Bazille, Whistler, Nadar, Astruc, Renoir, occasionally Degas, Monet, Cézanne, and Pissarro. But

his personality and his aims (if he had any other than simply to paint as well as he could) remain unclear. He was full of disingenuous advice to younger painters along the lines of "paint what you see as soon as you see it," but his technique was in a class of its own. Few artists could wield a brush with as much nervous energy and accuracy as Manet; few artists (apart from Degas) would dare to choose the subjects he did; few artists had the thorough grounding of five years at Couture's and countless hours copying in the great museums of Europe; few

MANET
Olympia
oil on canvas
1863. 130.5 × 190cm
(51 × 75in)
The older Courbet was critical of Olympia: "She looks like a Queen of Spades on a playing-card: not enough modelling." Manet, himself declared, "There is only one important thing: put down what you see the first time. If that's it, that's it." Manet painted with the light in his studio falling from behind him, which flattened the volumes of the figures in the painting, and brought the artist violent criticism.

MANET
Still Life with Peaches and Melon
oil on canvas
1866. 69 × 92cm (27 × 36in)
*ABOVE This again illustrates how
attached Manet was to tradition.
He painted a number of still lifes,
some with oysters, which were one
of the seventeenth-century Dutch
artists' favourite subjects. Manet's
work is never plagiaristic, no
more than was Bach's borrowing
of Vivaldi's musical themes.*

MANET
Madame Manet at the Piano
oil on canvas
c.1868. 38 × 46.5cm (15 × 18in)
*RIGHT Mme Manet was an
accomplished pianist, and the couple
often organized musical evenings
with their friends. Now a bourgeoise,
officially respectable since her
wedding, she accepted her husband's
passing affairs.*

artists had the leisure to paint (his
father had left him a more than
generous inheritance); ultimately
few of his contemporaries (except
Degas again) had the ineffable,
ambiguous sense of a picture that
Manet had. He was modest in
triumph, self-effacing in defeat and
did not have the inclination
of a Pissarro to teach. What
went through his mind is difficult
to discern.

However we do know that in
some respects Manet was highly
sensitive. In 1860 he moved his
studio to the rue Victoire after the
young boy who cleaned the
brushes and scraped the palettes for
him, the subject of *Child with
Cherries* (*L'Enfant aux cerises*),
hanged himself in the atelier,
inspiring a short story from
Baudelaire and sending Manet
into depression. The artist had
threatened to send the boy back to
his parents, but had not foreseen the

MANET
The Folkestone Boat, Boulogne
oil on canvas
1869. 60 × 73cm (24 × 29in)
*Manet spent the summer in
Boulogne with Degas, and painted
six landscapes, the only ones he
executed outside Paris in the 1860s.
The scene shows passengers about to
cross the English Channel.*

tragic effect of his reprimand. In the next two or three years as Manet's personal fame and ability to create scandal increased he found himself the subject of an irritable reprimand from Baudelaire. The poet had supported him loyally through the *Luncheon on the Grass* episode in 1863, but when the *Olympia* scandal erupted in 1865, Manet was at the end of his tether, desolated by the unheard of ferocity of the critics

towards him. The year before Baudelaire had drawn the artist's attention to the fact that *Agnes at Christ's Tomb* depicted the Saviour's spear wound on the wrong side of his body. He wrote to Manet: "You will have to change the position of the wound before the exhibition opens. And don't give those spiteful people a chance to laugh at you." During the *Olympia* scandal Manet wrote to Baudelaire in despair:

I wish you were here, my dear Baudelaire; they are raining insults on my head . . . I should have liked your sane verdict on my pictures, for all these cries have set me on edge . . . something must be wrong . . .

Baudelaire's withering rejoinder reads:

I am afraid I am again forced to speak to you about yourself. I shall have to apply myself to demonstrating to you just what your value is. What you ask is quite ridiculous. People are making fun of you, you say; their jokes set you on edge, etc, etc . . . Do you think you are the first man who has ever been in this position? Are you more of a genius than Chateaubriand or Wagner? Have people made fun of them, I wonder? They have not died of it. And in order not to inflate you with too much pride, I would add that these men are models, each in his own field, in a rich world, and that you, you are simply the foremost in the decrepitude of

MANET
Madame Manet and Her Son Léon at Arcachon
watercolour
1871.

A sketch of peaceful domesticity, the soothing atmosphere Manet needed to restore his shattered spirits. The crushing of the Commune had been merciless and bloody, and most people in Paris were affected by these tragic events.

MANET
Monet Painting in his
Studio Boat
oil on canvas
1874. 82.5 × 104cm
(33 × 41in)
*ABOVE Renoir and Monet spent
the summer of 1874 painting at
Argenteuil, then a small town
along the Seine, not very far from
Paris. Manet joined them and
produced four boating pictures.
It is certain that the younger
Monet influenced his style.*

MANET
Couple Boating
oil on canvas
1874. 97 × 130cm
(38 × 51in)
*RIGHT The man is his brother-in-
law Rodolphe Leenhoff, wearing
the outfit of a fashionable sailing
club. Manet showed the painting
at the Salon of 1879.*

your art. I do hope you won't take
this amiss. You know how dear you
are to me. I wanted to have M.
Chorner's personal impression
[of *Olympia* and *Christ Mocked*], at
least insofar as a Belgian can be
considered a person . . . What he
said tallies with what several
intelligent men have said about
you: "There are faults, weaknesses,
a lack of aplomb, but there is an
irresistible charm." I know all this,
I was the first to understand it. He
added that the picture of the nude,
the Negress and the cat (is it really
a cat?) was far superior to the
religious picture.

Manet's technique, as poor M.
Chorner observed, and Baudelaire
knew, was the least of his worries.
Since his years at Couture, when
he would draw objects perfectly but
upside down for fun, he had developed *peinture claire*, described by the
art historian Bernard Denvir as:

A method of painting . . . which
creates a high-key colour
configuration by first applying
loose-flowing and *grasse*, or fat,
pigment on to the canvas, and then
whilst the paint is still wet, adding
the half-tones and darker passages
. . . the reverse of the accepted
Academic process. The resulting
effect is one of sparkle and
vitality . . .

The problem for contemporary
critics was that he had applied this
bold and innovative technique to a
fundamental reinterpretation of
some of the icons of western art. By
reinventing the nude in *Luncheon on
the Grass* and *Olympia*, with explicit
reference to past masters, he had
appeared to rupture a series of
seemingly inviolable traditions. To
the budding Impressionists he was

MANET
The River at Argenteuil
oil on canvas
1874. 61 × 100cm (24 × 39in)
ABOVE Manet was much less interested in the effects of light than Monet and Renoir. Manet's brushwork is much smoother and more controlled than that of the other two artists.

MANET
The Monet Family in Their Garden
oil on canvas
1874. 61 × 100cm (24 × 39in)
RIGHT The Monets received the Manets and the Renoirs during the summer of 1874, and both artists painted the Monets in their garden. Mme Monet and her son Jean have such similar poses that the pictures seem to have been done at the same time.

MANET
Venice, the Grand Canal
oil on canvas
1875. 57 × 48cm (22 × 19in)
*LEFT Manet went to Venice
with Tissot, who had been
enjoying great success with his
elegant paintings in London
since the war. Manet's style now
shows the effect of his summer
in Argenteuil the previous year
and is much more impressionistic,
with shorter, choppier brushstrokes
and a heightened palette.*

MANET
Nana
oil on canvas
1877. 150 × 116cm
(59 × 46in)
*BELOW Nana did not scandalize the
public as much as Olympia had
previously, but the painting was also
refused by the jury of the Salon, for
much the same reasons. The model
was the actress Henriette Hauser,
mistress of the Prince of Orange.*

an iconoclast; to his own mind he was simply carrying on in the tradition he was falsely accused of breaking.

By the age of thirty-eight, and the outbreak of the Franco-Prussian War in 1870, Manet had painted several masterpieces and as Zola had said in 1866 in *L'Evénement*: "Our fathers laughed at M. Courbet so we went into raptures over his work. Now it is we who laugh at M. Manet and it is our children who will be in raptures at his canvases." Manet was now probably the most famous (and infamous) artist of his day, but by the end of the Commune his nerves were shattered and he went to Boulogne in August 1871 to recover. Despite his ubiquitous fame he had sold very few paintings in the 1860s. This was scarcely a problem financially, but his self-esteem demanded buyers for his work, and success at the Salon.

MANET
The Tub
pastel on canvas
1878–79. 54 × 45cm
(21 × 18in)
*BELOW Manet did not paint many
nudes, and this one is reminiscent of the
poses more familiar in his friend Degas'
work, although the approach is quite
different. The woman, like* Nana *and*
Olympia, *is aware of the gaze of either
the viewer or the painter, whereas
Degas's women are oblivious to any
presence near them.*

Durand-Ruel, the saviour of Monet, Pissarro, Renoir, and Sisley now stepped in and (with as great foresight as ever) bought 50,000 francs worth of paintings. Manet refused, however, to part with *Music in the Tuileries, Luncheon on the Grass, Olympia*, and *The Execution of Maximilian*, which Durand-Ruel had valued together at a total of 76,000 francs, an astronomical sum. *Olympia* was eventually purchased for the French nation by a subscription organized by Monet in 1890, seven years after Manet's death. For seventeen years the Louvre refused to hang the picture until Monet

sought the aid of Président Clemenceau in 1907 and had it transferred from the Musée de Luxembourg to the Louvre – the whiff of scandal lingered around the painting for decades.

In December 1874 Manet's close friend Berthe Morisot married his brother Eugène. Thereafter there were no more languorous paintings of her pictured as she is in *The Balcony* (*Le Balcon*) or *The Sofa*. Whatever their relationship had been before – it had certainly been intense – she sat for him no more. In 1876 Manet met Méry Laurent, on whom Marcel Proust's character Odette Swann was based, a formidable courtesan and the lover of the poet Stéphane Mallarmé. It is possible that Manet had an affair with her; certainly they were devoted to one another in the last years of his life and she is the subject of his

MANET
The Plum
oil on canvas
1878. 73.5 × 50cm (29 × 20in)
LEFT This young woman is holding an unlit cigarette and has ordered a plum in brandy. The picture shows the unique stillness of many of Manet's sitters. Various interpretations have been suggested, but she is probably just a working girl passing the time before she returns to her small lodgings.

last work. The Symbolist poet Mallarmé and Manet had become friends in 1873 and developed a close and constant friendship to rival that with the late Baudelaire. Mallarmé was far removed from the decadence of Baudelaire (who was forced to borrow money from Manet and still owed him 500 francs when he died). He held salons on Tuesday nights crammed with the literary and artistic lions of his day, including Manet and the Impressionists. Manet's association

MANET
Study for the Beer Waitress
oil on canvas
1878–79. 77.5 × 65cm
(31 × 26in)
ABOVE The model is a waitress Manet knew, but she would only pose in the presence of her boyfriend, who is seated. In this study, the woman is also aware of an external presence, and looks at us.

MANET
The Beer Waitress
oil on canvas
1878–79. 97 × 77.5cm
(38 × 31in)
LEFT Manet has enlarged the composition to place the two sitters in a wider environment, and we can see more of the performer on stage. The setting was the cabaret Reichshoffen, on the Boulevard de Rochechouart, but the painting was done in Manet's studio.

MANET
The Artist's Garden
oil on canvas
1881. 65 × 81cm
(26 × 32in)
ABOVE In bad health, Manet rented a villa in Versailles during the summer of 1881, intending to paint the classical gardens of the castle, but he was not able to fulfil his project.

with Mallarmé resulted in illustrations for the poet's translation of Edgar Allan Poe's *The Raven* as well as a remarkable portrait of Mallarmé which shows Manet under the increasing influence of his Impressionist friends. Indeed, the summer Manet had spent with Monet and his family at Argenteuil in 1874 had released his rather sombre style into a much more colourful, impressionistic idiom. His paintings of Monet, Camille, and Jean in the open air are some of the liveliest documents of the heyday of Impressionism. Manet's new-found

MANET
At the Café-concert
oil on canvas
1879. 47 × 39cm
(19 × 15in)
OPPOSITE Another café-concert scene with a young woman very similar to the sitter in The Plum, *who is also holding a cigarette. The man is like many characters of the time, not quite chic but of a relative bohemian elegance. We also find an example here of reflection in a mirror, which is most strikingly exploited in the later* Bar at the Folies-Bergère.

MANET
Study for Bar at the Folies-Bergère
oil on canvas
1881. 47 × 56cm
(19 × 22in)
*RIGHT In this large sketch, nearly
half the size of the finished work, the
waitress is off centre, looking sideways,
and the mirror seems to be immediately
behind her, while the male customer is
very small.*

MANET
Bar at the Folies-Bergère
oil on canvas
1881–82. 96 × 130cm (38 × 51in)
*ABOVE In the finished painting, Manet
returns to his instinctive preferences and
the waitress is facing us, but seems to
look through us rather than at us.
The foreground forms in itself a very
beautiful still life, but Manet was
much criticized for his handling of the
woman's back and the customer reflected
in the mirror. It is indeed inaccurate,
but does it matter?*

MANET
Portrait of Irma Brunner
pastel on canvas
1882. 53.5 × 44cm (21 × 17in)
LEFT The sitter was of Viennese origin and was introduced to Manet by his friend Méry Laurent in 1882. Manet liked profile portraits of women wearing dark hats, providing a strong background for the sitter's features.

MANET
Autumn (Méry Laurent)
oil on canvas
1881. 72 × 50cm (28 × 20in)

BELOW The sitter was Méry Laurent, a "grande cocotte" he had met in 1876 when she came to see the show he had set up in his studio after two of his paintings had been turned down by the Salon. It was a huge success, and people queued in the street to see. They were casual lovers and remained very good friends. This picture, commissioned by Antonin Proust, was to be one of four symbolizing the seasons, a theme which had been popular throughout the centuries, but Manet did not complete the series.

interest in light and colour continued to produce sparkling canvases when he visited Venice the next year.

By the end of the 1880s Manet was beginning to feel the effects of the disease locomotor ataxia, which was to kill him before long. The official recognition he so strongly desired was still eluding him; yet he was still capable of causing a stir. In 1876 *Nana* had been rejected by the Salon on the grounds of impropriety and in 1881 he was damned with faint praise when the Salon awarded him a *seconde médaille* for his *Portrait of Pertuiset*. Finally his childhood friend Antonin Proust, who had risen to the rank of Arts Minister, secured Manet the *Légion d'Honneur*. Although he was working flat out on his last masterpiece, the *Bar at the Folies-Bergère*, he was in considerable pain, finding it increasingly difficult to hold a paintbrush. On 6th April 1883 he could no longer walk and was confined to bed. Two weeks later his left leg was amputated to stop the spread of gangrene. He died on 30th April and was buried in Passy cemetery on 3rd May.

Degas

I N A FAMOUS STATEMENT, Edgar Degas likened his art to the perpetration of a crime; "make counterfeits," he said "and add a touch of nature." Degas never painted en *plein air* and had nothing but scorn for painters who did, preferring to make sketches of his subjects – primarily the human figure in motion – and use whatever means at his disposal, including photography, to ensure the accuracy of his observation before working in the studio. Thus, until his later experiments with pastel and gouache, Degas had very little to do with the Impressionism of Monet, Renoir, or even the later work of Manet. But, like Manet, his inspiration grew directly out of an intense admiration for past masters.

Despite his uncompromising refusal to espouse the style of his Impressionist colleagues, Degas was instrumental in the foundation of the *Société anonyme* and all the subsequent Impressionist exhibitions except one.

DEGAS
Self-portrait
c.1855.
ABOVE

DEGAS
Dancers at
the Barre
pastel on paper
c.1877.
66 × 51cm
(26 × 20in)
OPPOSITE

LIFE AND WORKS: EDGAR DEGAS (1834–1917)

A painting is a thing which requires as much trickery, malice, and vice as the perpetration of a crime; make counterfeits and add a touch of nature.

EDGAR DEGAS

Edgar Degas, like Manet, was born into the higher echelons of Parisian society; in fact he came into the world on 19th July 1834 above a branch of his family's Neapolitan bank in the rue Saint-Georges. But unlike Manet, Degas did not have to fight his parents to become an artist. Amongst the Degas' friends were several eminently wealthy art collectors and government officials who encouraged Edgar, already self-taught, by allowing him to study and copy their art treasures. The Valpinçons, for example, owned Ingres' *Odalisque au turban*, a source of enduring delight and inspiration to the young Degas; and Achille Devéria, Keeper of the Cabinet d'Estampes, the Prints and Drawings Room at the Bibliothèque Nationale, allowed Edgar to peruse the collections and copy the works in them. By the time he was eighteen Degas had also obtained permission to copy at the Louvre. In a comfortable family environment, free of untoward pressure, with a father devoted to him (his mother died when he was fifteen), Edgar Degas was able to indulge his talents with the help of the finest public and private collections in Paris. In 1854 he was to visit wealthy uncles, aunts, and cousins in Naples and Florence where, as one biographer puts it, he undertook an orgy of museums and copying the old masters – Raphael, Mantegna,

Bellini, Poliamolo, Botticelli, and Giotto. "Draw lines, young man, draw lines," Ingres is said to have advised his young devotee in 1855 when Edouard Valpinçon took Degas to visit the French master, and this he did, and continued to do.

By July 1856 Degas had finished his brief academic studies, having gained a place at the Ecole des Beaux-Arts the year before, studying with a disciple of Ingres, Louis Lamothe. Degas' ability was by now considerable; deep immersion in old masters of every conceivable school, but particularly the Italians, was producing polished results. He then set off for an extended tour of Italy which lasted until April 1859, where he continued to devour the old masters and paint family portraits. In November 1858 Degas' father Auguste, having just received a packing case from his son, wrote to him in Florence with some pride:

I have unrolled your paintings and some of your drawings. I was very pleased, and I can tell you that you have taken a great step forward in your art; your drawing is strong, the colours are right. You have rid yourself of the weak, trivial, Flandrinian, Lamothian manner of drawing and that dull grey colour. My dear Edgar, you have no reason to go on tormenting yourself, you are on the right track . . . You have a great destiny ahead of you . . .

INGRES
Odalisque
oil on canvas
1826. 32 × 25cm
(13 × 10in)
This is the purity of line the young Degas admired. Friends of the Degas family had an odalisque similar to this, which fascinated the young Degas.

Auguste Degas seems to have had the measure of his son's potential; the portraits, self-portraits, genre paintings, copies of frescos and old masters produced in Degas' youth bespoke a solid if somewhat unexciting future for the artist. The abundance of self-portraits at such an early age testifies to Degas' single-minded obsession not only with art, but with himself; he resolutely remained a bachelor for the rest of his life.

On his return to Paris, Degas continued his steady self-improvement by copying in the Louvre, gaining permission to do so by listing his friend Emile Lévy as his fictitious master. That was where

Edouard Manet first met him in 1862, interrupting him in the process of copying Velazquez's *Infanta Margarita* on to a copper plate. At this time Degas was trying to finish his first important history painting, *Semiramis Building Babylon*, and, with the usual friendly rivalry which marked their relationship, Manet was to jest a decade later in the Café de la Nouvelle-Athène that "Degas was painting Semiramis when I was painting modern Paris." Manet had certainly completed *The Absinthe Drinker, Music in the Tuileries Gardens*, and the epochal *Luncheon on the Grass* by this time and was practically re-inventing art, as his critics saw it, but Degas, only two

DEGAS
Young Spartans
oil on canvas
c.1860. 109 × 154.5cm
(43 × 61in)
Degas was inspired by his reading of classical authors for this unusual subject. In contrast to more academic painters, he deliberately left out classical elements such as Greek buildings.

DEGAS
On the Cliff-top
pastel on paper
c.1869. 30.5 × 45cm
(12 × 18in)
*Although Degas was a virulent
anti-*plein-airiste, *he painted
around a hundred landscapes
in brief periods during the 1860s
and the 1890s.*

DEGAS
Races in the Country
oil on canvas
1869. 36.5 × 56cm (14 × 22in)
This is a portrait of Degas'
boyhood friend Paul Valpinçon,
with his wife leaning over the
nurse who holds their new-born
son. Degas did several portraits of
his friend and family, and often
stayed with them in Normandy.

DEGAS
Manet Listening to His Wife
Playing the Piano
oil on canvas
1865. 65 × 71cm (26 × 28in)
*ABOVE Manet did not like the
way Degas had depicted his wife
Suzanne in this double portrait,
and cut part of the canvas off,
much to Degas' horror. Degas
intended to restore it but never
did, perhaps because Manet
executed a similar portrait
later on.*

DEGAS
The Dance Class
oil on canvas
c. 1874. 83.5 × 77cm (33 × 30in)
*OPPOSITE Degas' dance pictures are
set in the old Opera House, which
burnt down in 1873. He made
numerous studies of the dancers.*

years younger than Manet, was not far behind: *The Gentleman's Race: Before the Start*, with its highly original composition, dates from 1862.

The relationship between the two artists is described in several tantalizing anecdotes by their friends (and enemies), but remains clouded in a certain amount of mystery. We do know that they admired each other greatly and were in frequent contact; at one point in 1869, for example, Manet wrote to Degas asking for the return of two volumes of Baudelaire. One incident in particular tells us a great deal about their strange relationship. Between 1868 and 1869 Degas painted a double portrait of Manet with his wife, Suzanne, at the piano. It survives with a piece of canvas attached to the place where half of Mme Manet used to be before M. Manet slashed it off in a fit of pique. In 1924, with dubious accuracy, but with much wit, the dealer Ambroise Vollard recounted the tale Degas had told him in this way:

Vollard: Who slashed that painting?
Degas: To think it was Manet who did that! He thought that something about Mme Manet wasn't right. Well . . . I'm going to try to restore Mme Manet, What a shock I had when I saw it at Manet's . . . I left without saying goodbye, taking my picture with me. When I got home I took down a little still life he had given me. "Monsieur," I wrote, "I am returning your *Plums*."

Vollard: But you saw each other again afterwards?
Degas: How could you expect anyone to stay on bad terms with Manet?

By the early 1870s Degas had emerged from his deep and intensive involvement in the past and its forms and, following the example of Manet, he was beginning to apply himself to painting the world of modern Paris, in particular its people (and horses) in motion. Unlike the Impressionists with whom he was to be deeply involved, Degas had shown little interest in landscape. Vollard remembers him wryly pronouncing: "If I were the government, I would have a squad of gendarmes to keep an eye on these people painting landscapes from nature. Oh! I don't wish anyone dead. I would, however, agree to spraying them with a little bird-shot, for starters!" But the landscapes he produced in the late 1860s are delicate, imaginary pastels done in the studio, whilst the monotypes of the 1890s are even more imaginary, appearing almost completely abstract.

The range of the subjects he tackled in the ensuing years is formidable: ballet dancers in rehearsal and before, during, and after performance; racehorses – before, during, and after the race; café-concerts and their singers in performance; the opera; acrobats; prostitutes; businessmen; milliners; a pedicurist, musicians; a billiard room. No nook or cranny of Paris in the 1870s and 1880s was immune from his fastidious gaze or

DEGAS
Aux Ambassadeurs
pastel/monotype
1877. 37 × 27cm
(15 × 11in)
*ABOVE Degas started to make mono-
types towards the mid-1870s. The
process consists of applying greasy
printer's ink or oil paint on a metal
plate. The plate is then printed on
paper and can be coloured with a
variety of media, mainly oil or pastel.
Café-concerts were a favourite haunt
of Parisians, and they varied in price
and quality.*

DEGAS
The Absinthe Drinker
oil on canvas
1875–76. 92 × 68cm
(36 × 27in)
*OPPOSITE The sitters are the actress
Ellen Andrée and the painter
Marcellin Desboutin, both friends
of Degas. When Walter Crane
saw it in 1893, he said it was
a study in human degradation,
male and female.*

his notebook. These notebooks,
which have survived, allow us an
important insight into the artist's
mind. "Draw all kinds of everyday
objects," reads a note from 1876,
"placed, accompanied in such a way
that they have in them the life of
the man or woman – corsets which
have just been removed, for
example, and which retain the
form of the body, etc, etc." Another
note reads:

> On bakery, *Bread* – series on
> baker's boys, seen in the cellar
> itself, or through the basement
> window from the street – backs
> the colour of pink flour –
> beautiful curves of dough – still
> lives of different breads, large, oval,
> round, etc. Studies in colour of
> the yellows, pinks, greys, whites
> of bread . . . 2 panels on birth –
> delicate mother, fashionable – food
> – large wet-nurse – large behind –
> enormous ribbons. Lilac coloured
> dress fluted like a pillar . . .

He had inherited both the dark and
corrupting Paris of Baudelaire with
its accursed denizens –

> *You who wander, stoic,*
> *without complaint,*
> *Across the chaos of the living city,*
> *Mothers with bleeding hearts,*
> *courtesanes or saints,*
> *Whose names in former times were on*
> *the lips of all . . .*

(from *Les Fleurs du Mal*)

– and the sparkling life of *la ville
lumière*, the only place he really felt
at home, with its ordinary working
people, its ever–increasing number
of cafés, concerts, operas and ballets,
stars and starlets.

DEGAS
Portraits at the Stock Exchange
oil on canvas
c.1878–79. 100 × 82cm
(39 × 32in)
ABOVE

DEGAS
Edmond Duranty
pastel and tempera on paper
1879. 101 × 100.5cm (40 × 40in)
*ABOVE Duranty was a wealthy literary
and art critic. Degas made three
preliminary drawings for this picture,
which was executed a year before
Duranty's death.*

DEGAS
The Name Day of the Madam
pastel/monotype
1876–77. 26.5 × 29.5cm
(10 × 12in)
*RIGHT It is easy to believe that Degas
made these pictures for his own and
his friends' amusement. The same
was probably true of Picasso, who
owned this picture.*

Above all Degas was concerned with the female form: women dancing, women singing, women ironing, women before, during, and after the bath, women sleeping, combing and braiding their hair.

Degas has another comprehension of life, a different concern for exactitude before nature. There is certainly a woman there, but a certain kind of woman, *without the expression of a face*, without the wink of an eye, without the décor of the *toilette*, a woman reduced to the gesticulation of her limbs, to the appearance of her body, a woman considered as a female, expressed in her animality . . .

This is what the contemporary critic Gustave Geffroy thought of Degas' female subjects. It underlines the profound difference between Degas and Manet, who had presented the female nude and the semi-dressed *Nana* as provocations to accepted notions of art. Similarly Degas' late nudes bear only a passing resemblance to Renoir's in their rotundity. Renoir depicts his women "*with the expression of a face*", and all that implies, increasingly Degas' women at their toilette are, as the 1890s wear on, studies of line and colour; indeed the coloured line, possible with pastels,

DEGAS
Brothel Inmates
pastel/monotype
c.1879. 14 × 20.5cm
(6 × 8in)
Degas did about fifty such works, which have always puzzled his admirers and critics as well as scholars, who offer various interpretations for this choice of subject and the manner in which it is treated.

DEGAS
Nude Combing Her Hair
pastel/monotype
c.1877–79. 21.5 × 16cm (9 × 6in)
ABOVE It is indeed paradoxical that the admirer of Ingres' pure and idealized figures could produce such pictures.

DEGAS
Study for Miss La La at
the Cirque Fernando
pastel on paper
1879. 61 × 48cm (24 × 19in)
RIGHT Degas attended performances at the circus in January 1879, and made several studies, of which this is the last.

DEGAS
Miss La La at the Cirque Fernando
oil on canvas
1879. 117 × 77.5cm
(46 × 31in)
OPPOSITE The cirque Fernando was located in Montmartre and later became the Medrano circus. As for Miss La La, she was renowned for the strength of her teeth.

opened up new avenues for experimentation. As he put it to Sickert, "They [his contemporaries, the Impressionists] are all exploiting the possibilities of colour. And I am always begging them to exploit the possibilities of drawing. It is the richer field." And none could draw with the mastery, and ultimately the abandonment, of Degas.

Degas' sheer energy, his urge to capture fleeting movement in its countless nuances resulted in a prodigious series of paintings, pastels, monotypes, drawings and eventually wax sculpture. Apart from the portraits it is almost impossible to find a Degas where movement and action are not inherent, yet his method was the exact opposite of the Impressionists. He did not attempt to capture the moment in a quick stroke of the brush – there is nothing impulsive about Degas. Everything is studied, planned and executed in the studio in controlled conditions – "I assure you no art is less spontaneous than mine. What I do is the result of reflection and study of the great

DEGAS
Women Ironing
oil on canvas
c.1884–86. 76 × 81cm
(30 × 32in)
*ABOVE The contemporary critic and
friend of the impressionists Georges
Rivière wrote about Degas: "he is an
observer, he never seeks exaggeration.
The effect is always obtained from
nature herself, without caricature.
This is what makes him the most
valuable historian of the scene he
shows us.*

DEGAS
The Millinery Shop
oil on canvas
c.1882–86. 100 × 110.5cm
(39 × 44in)
*RIGHT This is the largest of a series
characterized by its unusual and
ingenious compositions.*

masters. Of inspiration, spontaneity,
temperament, I know nothing." On
another occasion and on a slightly
different note he said: "It is all very
well to copy what one sees, but
it is much better to draw what
one remembers. A transformation
results in which imagination
collaborates with memory. You will
reproduce only what is striking,
which is to say, only what is
necessary. That way, your memories
and your fantasies are liberated from
the tyranny of nature."

Degas approached his involvement with the Impressionists from
the point of view of a Realist
because he considered himself to be
one and saw the first Impressionist
exhibition in the rue des Capucines
as an opportunity to promote what
he called "a Salon of Realists." It
should be noted that the terms
Realism and Naturalism were
confused and interchangeable at the
time. Realists–Naturalists could also
be Impressionists as far as the critics
of the day were concerned; the
term Impressionism subsumed a
great deal that was deemed to be
new or revolutionary. Thus Degas
and Manet, by virtue of their age
and status, were wrongly thought to
be leaders of the Impressionist
movement, when these titles have
been awarded to Monet and
Pissarro. It is clear that Degas had
no interest in the *plein-airisme*
being explored by Monet, Pissarro,
Renoir, Sisley, and Morisot in
the 1870s; his subjects were exclusively Parisian, from racehorses to
prostitutes. Moreover, he was
experimenting with new techniques and revitalizing neglected
media such as pastel, gouache, and

DEGAS
Woman Drying Her Foot
pastel on buff paper
c.1885–86. 54.5 × 52.5cm
(22 × 21in)
*ABOVE Degas painted numerous bathing
scenes, and asked his models to adopt a
great variety of poses. Of drawing, he
said: "Drawing is not form, it is the
sensation one has of it." And:
"Drawing is not what one sees but
what one can make others see."*

DEGAS
Ballerina and Lady with a Fan
pastel on paper
1885. 66 × 51cm (26 × 20in)
*OPPOSITE This is a good example of
Degas' sophisticated compositions: the
woman in the foreground with her fan
is in the shadow while the dancer is
brightly lit. In the background, as in a
framed photograph, fragmentary
dancers rendered in subdued tones do
not distract from the star.*

even distemper (used for painting
scenery) in an attempt to transcend
what were now appearing to be the
limitations of oil paint. Abandoning
oils meant he could paint rapidly on
a paper support which could be
infinitely extended by sticking
separate pieces of paper together as
required. In another vein he was
experimenting with alternatives to
the traditional gilt frames. Having
revolutionized the framing of
subjects within the composition, he
now addressed himself to the
immediate environment of the
picture, even including the décor
and lighting of the exhibition
room itself.

Degas' interest in modern life
embraced not only those who lived
it but also the technological
innovations of his day, from a new
electric method of drypoint
etching to Eadweard Muybridge's
extraordinary photographic discoveries about the nature of human
and animal locomotion. Degas
himself was a keen photographer.
Manet and the Impressionists had
all been influenced to varying
degrees by the new window on the
world photography offered, but
Degas, the scientific Realist,
absorbed Muybridge's discoveries
with particular relish.

In 1872 Muybridge, an
Englishman working for the
U.S. government, had begun to
experiment with a photographic
process which captured the
movement of a horse in motion in
order to discover whether all
four hoofs left the ground simulta-
neously during the trot, canter, and
gallop. With the financial assistance
of Leland Stanford, the Governor

DEGAS
Jockeys
oil on paper
c.1886–90. 26 × 36cm
(10 × 14in)
Race horses are a subject to which Degas frequently returned throughout his career. They are usually depicted just before or after the race itself, allowing for a variety of movement. Degas was an intense observer and had a well trained visual memory which enabled him to produce all these works in his studio, using notes made at the scene of the action.

DEGAS
Self-portrait with his Housekeeper
Zöe Closier
photographic self-portrait
1898–1900.
Degas had used photography
for his work since 1865.

of California, Muybridge eventually succeeded, between 1877 and
1878, in using a battery of cameras
and trip wires to expose frames at
one thousandth of a second of a
moving horse thus settling the
argument once and for all. The first
news of Muybridge's experiments
had reached Paris as early as 1874
but until the publication of
Muybridge's *Animal Locomotion* in
1887, the punctilious Degas was still
drawing his horses' gait in the
received manner, which is to say
incorrectly. Degas set about
studying and making pastel copies
of Muybridge's photographs and
after 1887 his horses all show the
influence of the new information,
including a series of wax sculptures
of horses jumping and rearing.

In his personal life Degas was a
confirmed bachelor, but a devoted
friend to those who could conquer
the barrier of prickliness he erected
around himself. His relationship to

the Impressionists was marked by an
energetic involvement in their
cause, even though he himself was
uninterested in *plein-airisme* as such.
Like Renoir, he was profoundly
anti-Semitic and sided vociferously
with the anti-Dreyfusards, even
though he worked closely with
Pissarro and his childhood friend,
the novelist and dramatist, Ludovic
Halévy. In his last years his eyesight,
which had troubled him all his life,
began to fail. "Since my eyesight has
diminished further my twilight has
become more and more lonely and
more and more sombre. Only the
taste for art and the desire to
succeed keep me going," he wrote
in the last years of the century.
He kept going until his death
on 27th September 1917, turning
increasingly to sculpture to express
himself and producing, ironically,
in his last years, his most
impressionistic and colourful works
in pastel.

DEGAS
Three Russian Dancers
pastel on paper
c.1910. 62 × 67cm (24 × 26in)
Degas produced a series of about
seventeen Russian dancers, of which
this is probably a later example. Some
of the others are more colourful.

T HE NAMES OF CLAUDE MONET and Impressionism are nearly synonymous. It was, after all, one of his paintings that gave the movement its title, and he was the most consistent, the most prolific and the most uncompromising of his generation in the struggle to capture the transitory effect – the attempt to depict the totality of the motif before him. There was never enough of anything for him: enough of the right quality of light, enough money, enough time, enough appreciation. To be a friend of Monet in the early days meant a drain on one's financial and emotional resources, as the kindly Bazille discovered. However, in the last few decades of world-wide success and lionization, the once impecunious painter of "tongue-lickings" was fetching thousands of dollars for a painting of a grain-stack, and he made sure that he was not undercut, juggling dealers to get the right price.

RENOIR
Claude Monet
1875.
ABOVE

MONET
Walk in the
Country
oil on canvas
1875.
60 × 80cm
(24 × 32in)
OPPOSITE

Life and Works: Claude Monet (1840–1926)

. . . the more I go on, the more I see that a lot of work has to be done in order to render what I seek: "instantaneity", above all the enveloppe*, the same light spreading everywhere and more than ever I am disgusted by easy things that come without effort . . .*

Letter from Monet to Gustave Geffroy, 21st July 1890

Claude Oscar Monet, the youngest of two sons, was born on 14th November 1840 in Paris. Five years later Adolphe Monet took his family to live in Le Hâvre, a seaport on the Normandy coast, where he joined the busy firm of wholesalers and ship's chandlers run by his relations, the Lecadres. At an early age Claude showed an aptitude for drawing and when he was old enough to attend the Collège du Hâvre he began to study under the eye of Charles Ochard who himself had studied under the great Neo-Classicist, and painter-advocate to Emperor Napoleon I, Jacques-Louis David.

"I more or less lived the life of a vagabond," said Monet in 1900 recalling his early years. "By nature I was undisciplined; never, even as a child, would I submit to rules. It was at home that I learned the little I know. School seemed like a prison and I could never bear to stay there, even for four hours a day, especially when the sunshine beckoned and the sea was smooth." By the age of fifteen Monet was by his own account known all over Le Hâvre as

a caricaturist, a pastime he had developed by drawing caricatures of his teachers "in the most irreverent fashion." However the more serious side of his talent was encouraged by his aunt, Mme Lecadre, an amateur painter who took Claude's artistic development to heart, especially after the death of his mother in 1857. Monet's devotion to art worsened his relationship with his father who wanted Claude to stay at school and take his baccalaureate. Mme Lecadre was acquainted with the painter Armand Gautier and together they persuaded the reluctant Adolphe Monet to let his son pursue a career in art. Thus the young Monet got his own way and skipped the examination, leaving school with no qualifications save an abundance of energy and an uncompromising belief in himself.

Monet's talents needed to be channelled in the right direction, however; he could not be expected to progress in the art world without formal training of some sort, although this was much against his nature. An early turning point came when Gravier, the frame-maker, in

MONET
View of Rouelles
oil on canvas
1858. 46 × 65cm (18 × 26in)
*Believed to be the first of Monet's
landscapes. We find in this corner of*

*Normandy some of the themes that
would later dominate Monet's work:
water, poplars and a good deal of sky.
Boudin had introduced him to open-air
painting about two years previously.*

JONGKIND
Fire on the Pont Neuf, Paris
oil on canvas
1853. 27.5 × 40.7cm
(11 × 16in)
*ABOVE Jongkind and Boudin were
Monet's real masters, and the
younger painter was not in
the least shaken when both
were rejected by the Salon.*

MONET
Still Life with Bottles
oil on canvas
1859. 41 × 60cm
(16 × 24in)
*OPPOSITE BOTTOM Still lifes and
nude studies were very much part
of an artist's training and Monet,
who rarely depicted this kind of
subject, shows that he could already
produce solid if not exceptional
studies. A short while later,
Troyon encouraged him to
practise drawing.*

whose shop Monet often displayed his drawings, introduced him to the local landscapist Eugène Boudin. Monet had been avoiding this meeting – he thought Boudin's landscapes were "horrible, used as I was to the false and arbitrary colour and fantastic arrangements of the painters then in vogue" – but Boudin eventually persuaded Monet to accompany him on a landscape expedition. It was a revelation: "I understood," said Monet, "I had seen what painting could be, simply by the example of this painter working with such independence at the art he loved. My destiny as a painter was decided."

Having failed to obtain a grant to study art in Paris from the municipal authorities in Le Hâvre, Monet gathered up his savings – income from the caricatures – and

went to Paris in the spring of 1859 armed with letters of introduction from Boudin to several artists including Troyon and Gautier. Troyon thought Monet showed promise and advised him to enrol at Thomas Couture's atelier (where Edouard Manet had studied). Monet dismissed this idea out of hand, even though Couture was known to be one of the more enlightened masters in Paris at the time, and returned to Le Hâvre. He was back in Paris again the next winter drawing the models at the free Académie Suisse, where his first encounter with Pissarro took place.

In 1861 Monet was called up for military service (which normally lasted seven years). Young men had to submit their names and be selected by chance. Families with the means, however, could buy their sons out of the lottery. Adolphe offered to do this if Monet would renounce art and join the family business. Instead, Monet defiantly enlisted. He joined the Chasseurs d'Afrique in the French colony of Algeria (where he was deeply impressed by the qualities of light and space), but was home within a year suffering from typhoid. It was then that he met his first "true master . . . the final education of my eye," Johan Jongkind, a Dutch land- and seascapist who was to prove a seminal influence.

Mme Lecadre, who was convinced of Monet's potential, offered to buy him out of the army and a deal was struck with Adolphe whereby Monet would go to Paris with an allowance to study art on the condition that he joined a recognized atelier and undertook

MONET
Route de Chailly, Fontainebleau
oil on canvas
1864. 98 × 129cm
(39 × 51in)
ABOVE *Chailly was a village near
Barbizon, dear to the landscapists
of the previous generation such
as Corot, Courbet and Daubigny.
Monet wrote to Bazille about one
of his Fontainebleau landscapes,
saying that it might remind people
of Corot, but insisted that it was
not a deliberate attempt to copy
the style of the older artist.*

MONET
Farmyard in Normandy
oil on canvas
1864. 65 × 81.5cm (26 × 32in)
ABOVE In the summer of 1864, Monet travelled with Bazille down the Seine to Normandy, where they rented cheap lodgings and worked on landscapes before joining Jongkind and Boudin at Honfleur.

MONET
Luncheon on the Grass
oil on canvas
1865–66 (fragment).
248 × 217cm (98 × 85in)
OPPOSITE Spurred by Manet's recent and infamous Luncheon on the Grass, Monet decided to paint his own version of the subject, which he did as a plainly contemporary scene, using his friends as models, including his girlfriend Camille. We see the concern of the artist for clothes, but mainly for light, which falls from behind the figures and is rendered in bold patches. Monet said later that this picture marked the beginnings of his experiment with the principle of the division of colours, working at effects of light and colour which ran counter to accepted conventions.

formal tuition. Monet agreed and chose Charles Gleyre's atelier. Gleyre was noted for his interest in landscape and had trained many students for the Prix de Paysage Historique. He also charged only for models and equipment, not his teaching, which was an added incentive to Monet, whose father thought him irresponsible with money and was keeping him under tight financial reins.

Thus it was in 1862 that he began his studies at Gleyre's atelier and met Renoir, Bazille, and Sisley and within months was leading them off on landscape painting expeditions to the Fontainebleau Forest and the countryside around Paris. By 1863 French art was in turmoil; Edouard Manet had outraged visitors to the Salon des Refusés with his *Luncheon on the Grass* (*Déjeuner sur l'herbe*). Unknown and unnoticed, Monet was forging ahead with his own programme of energetic self-improvement, having rejected Gleyre's teaching. When Gleyre was forced to retire in 1864 Monet was twenty-four and at liberty to pursue his career as he saw fit, though still at the mercy of his father on whom he relied greatly for financial support. Bazille began to help out with money, companionship and by sharing a studio with him between 1865 and 1866, in the rue Furstenberg. Bazille's untimely death in the Franco-Prussian War was a grave blow to Monet.

By the Salon of 1865 Monet had enjoyed some limited success and gained a few commissions. That year the Salon accepted and exhibited two of his landscapes

to a mixed reception. One critic thought him "a young Realist who promises much," another compared his work to a child's scrawl. Despite the critics, the artist's intense engagement with the effects of light and colour was clearly emerging as Monet's focus: he was still under the influence of Boudin, Jongkind, Manet, and even Courbet, although his work showed no sign of turning into overt Realism. Monet's experiments with large-scale figure paintings at this time are the beginning of the end of his interest in people as a subject for painting. His own *Luncheon on the Grass* which was never completed was to have been a major integration of light effects and figures in a total composition which would, as Forge says, "monumentalize the language of a *plein-air* sketch."

It was an audacious attempt doomed perhaps to failure. Monet had neither the time, the studio space nor the money to devote himself to its completion. In 1865 he had injured his leg and was laid up for some time, unable to work on the painting. Bazille, who had abandoned his medical studies to become a painter, made good use of his medical skills and rigged up a contraption which dripped water on to Monet's leg to ease the pain. A touching portrait by Bazille shows an irritated Monet lying in bed at the Cheval-Blanc Inn in Chailly where he had spent the summer working on the ambitious picture, impatient for Bazille to come and model. Bazille's *Monet after His Accident* (*Monet après son accident*) is also an eloquent testimony

MONET
Cliffs at Etretat
oil on canvas
c.1868. 81 × 100cm (32 × 39in)
LEFT Etretat is further down the coast, and was to become one of Monet's favourite subjects. He painted this particular stretch of cliff called the Needle many times. In this early example, Monet parallels the strata of the stone with those of the sky.

MONET
Terrace at Sainte-Adresse
oil on canvas
1866–67. 98 × 129cm (39 × 51in)
BELOW In 1866 Monet was forced to leave Camille and go to his aunt's summer house at Sainte-Adresse, where he painted this view from a first-floor window. His aunt is barely seen under her parasol, and his father sits on the right. His cousin Jeanne-Marguerite stands with a friend by the trellis. Monet has left most of the sea empty to suggest depth, leaving a variety of ships to furnish the horizon.

MONET
Beach at Honfleur
oil on canvas
c.1867. 60 × 81cm (24 × 32in)
ABOVE Monet took full advantage of this summer to travel down the coast, painting a series of beach scenes in which one of his main preoccupations was the variable aspect of the light on the sea and in the sky. It is now impossible to mistake his work for that of Boudin, Jongkind or any other painter.

MONET
Zaandam
oil on canvas
1871. 40 × 72cm (16 × 28in)
ABOVE Leaving London, Monet went to the Netherlands, where he painted a series of landscapes in Zaandam and other sites. Holland was a natural choice for an artist so fond of water.

to the devotion of Bazille to his awkward friend.

Monet was in increasing trouble with his father and Aunt Lecadre. He had a girlfriend, Camille-Léonie Doncieux, who had posed for several figures in *Luncheon on the Grass* and a new large-scale picture, which was ultimately rejected by the Salon, *Women in the Garden (Femmes dans un jardin)*. The lovers fell foul of their respective parents. In 1867, Monet was being chased by creditors, Camille was pregnant and the 800 francs Monet had made from the Salon of 1866 had long

since run out. Aunt Lecadre, in league with Adolphe Monet, forced Claude to retreat to Sainte-Adresse on the Normandy coast. In his absence Monet's son Jean was born that July in Paris. We know from a letter Monet sent to Bazille in May 1867 that Camille herself was "ill, bedridden and penniless" and that he did not know what to do, except remind his friend he owed him fifty francs by the first of the month. Bazille had come to Monet's rescue by buying *Women in the Garden* for 2,500 francs to be paid in monthly instalments. In June he was asking Bazille for 100 or 150 francs; by

MONET
Bathers at La Grenouillère
oil on canvas
1869. 73 × 92cm (29 × 36in)
OPPOSITE BOTTOM *La Grenouillère was
so popular that even the Imperial couple
once stopped to visit it. Set on a small
island on the Seine, it consisted of two
barges moored under trees and roofed
with awnings. Gangplanks linked the
barges to a tiny artificial islet nick-
named the "camembert". The series of
paintings of La Grenouillère marks a
turning point in Impressionism,
although Monet thought that he had
only produced "rotten sketches".*

August he was writing a pitiful
letter to Bazille saying how much it
pained him to think of his child's
mother having nothing to eat. The
letter ends on a desperate demand
from Monet – "Really, Bazille," he
says, "there are things that can't be
put off until tomorrow. This is one
of them and I'm waiting."

The enforced sojourn at
Sainte-Adresse enabled Monet to
produce several beach scenes which
showed an increasing maturity of
vision. Sadly the whole episode
contributed to more disaster. In the
autumn Monet was suffering from
eye-strain caused by the brilliant

MONET
The Thames Below Westminster
oil on canvas
1871. 47 × 72.5cm (19 × 29in)
ABOVE *During the war Pissarro busied
himself in the area south of the Thames
where his mother lived. Monet stayed in
town, painting views of the parks, but
mainly the Thames, to which he often
returned in later years, especially in the
winter. He was fascinated by the effect
of light and fog unique to London, and
said that London would be ugly without
it. While he was there, he tried to exhibit
at the annual show of the Royal
Academy but was rejected.*

MONET
Poppy Field
oil on canvas
1873. 50 × 65cm (20 × 26in)
ABOVE This is almost certainly Camille and Jean walking in the tall grass of a field not far away from their home. This is the archetypal Impressionist painting – atmospheric, sketchy, lively, and full of light.

sunlight at Sainte-Adresse and was obliged to stop painting during that season. The next year, despite selling a full-length (and very sober) portrait of Camille called *Woman in the Green Dress (Femme en vert)* to the editor of *L'Artiste*, Arsène Houssaye, as well as a commission for a portrait of Mme Gaudibert, the wife of a Le Hâvre notable, Monet had his paintings seized by creditors at an exhibition in Le Hâvre. The strain on his relationship with Camille, who had a new baby to look after, must have been severe. The bad times rapidly alternated with the good. In June 1868 Monet, Camille, and Jean had been thrown out of a country inn; Monet had attempted suicide and said so to Bazille in a letter. Whether the hardy Norman was capable of

suicide is obscure – his liberal use of bathos in all his begging letters to Bazille is obvious. By December Monet was ecstatic; he wrote to Bazille from Etretat on the Normandy coast where he and his family were installed in a little cottage thanks to the patronage of M. Gaudibert, saying how happy he was surrounded by his family and able to work in peace. He adds with reference to his work: "The further I get the more I realize that no one ever dares give frank expression to what they feel."

In the summer of 1869 this is exactly what Monet began to do in earnest when, working in the company of Renoir at La Grenouillère on the Seine, he produced what are the first truly Impressionist paintings. Monet

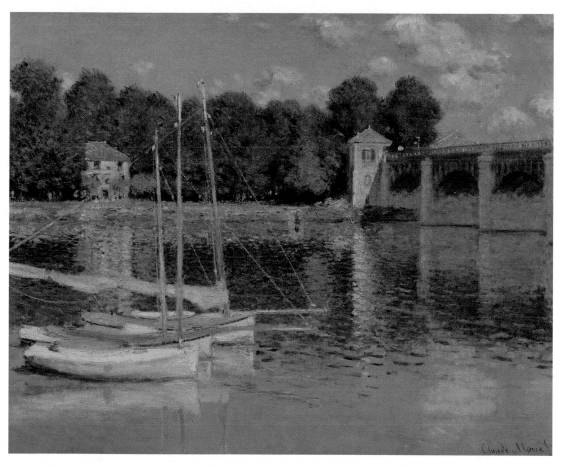

called them "rotten sketches" but signed them nonetheless. They were indeed sketches for a finished work which is now lost (but survives in a rather indistinct photograph) and which appears to show the existing Grenouillère pictures are not dissimilar to the completed version. At this point in the history of Impressionism in general, the distinction between sketch and completion was beginning to lose its importance. Monet was now using paint with increasing confidence in swift, bold brush-strokes, painting wet-in-wet in

MONET
Train in the Snow
oil on canvas
1875.
OPPOSITE BOTTOM Monet's house was opposite the station at Argenteuil, and he pictured it several times. This is one of many snow scenes, a subject he never tired of depicting, even if he had to endure the most appalling conditions.

MONET
The Bridge at Argenteuil
oil on canvas
1874. 60 × 81cm
(24 × 32in)
ABOVE Argenteuil had much to offer a painter like Monet: open country, a garden full of flowers, the Seine with its pleasure boats. The new bridge, rebuilt after the war, and the train, were modern elements which interested the Impressionists, in contrast to the Barbizon landscapists of the previous generation.

MONET
Gare St Lazare
oil on canvas
1877. 75.5 × 104cm
(30 × 41in)
A view of the famous station,
with the Pont de l'Europe
in the distance.

of his life despite many ups and downs. London itself – its mercurial climate, prodigious mists and fog, its river, parks and buildings – provided a new set of atmospheric problems for Monet to solve. He was to rediscover the vagaries of English weather to his delight and horror when he returned to London over thirty years later.

In 1871, after the war and the Commune, Monet returned to France and set up home with his family in Argenteuil on the Seine near Paris. There they remained in occasionally frugal stability for seven years. Settled in the growing but as yet rural town of Argenteuil, but near enough to Paris to make possible frequent trips there on the railway, Monet could now concentrate on transferring to the canvas the *enveloppe* which his unique vision disclosed. The subjects that now fell within his view ranged from Argenteuil and Paris streets, to the river and the railway, as well as his house and the surrounding countryside. Working out of doors whenever possible, Monet began the system which was to serve him until his death of having several canvases on the go at once, always ready to capture some fleeting atmospheric effect. He began to produce more varied views of the same subject as seen in different weather conditions. These culminate in his last Paris pictures – the series of Gare St Lazare paintings which treat the station, its massive structure and swirling clouds of steam as intricate webs of colour, truly urban landscapes.

places to create fluid and subtle mixtures of colour. This technique was developed in the work produced the next summer in Trouville on the Normandy coast, and reached new heights during his exile in London of 1870–71 and his subsequent trip to Holland.

Monet had just married Camille when he had to flee to London to avoid being called up to fight the Prussians. Although his time in London was fraught with difficulties – "I endured much poverty," he recalled in 1900 – it meant he was in the company of Pissarro, Daubigny, and the dealer Paul Durand-Ruel, all exiles from the war. The all-important business relationship he struck up there with Durand-Ruel was to last the rest

It is perhaps fitting that it was a picture by Monet, *Impression, Sunrise*, which gave the Impressionists their name, for during the 1870s he forged tirelessly ahead and came to exert a powerful influence on his fellow artists. Edouard Manet's summer season at Argenteuil alongside Monet resulted in Manet's decisive shift towards the Impressionist style of swiftly applied bright pigment. Renoir and Pissarro were also visitors to Argenteuil. For a relatively brief period Monet was at the heart of the Impressionist enterprise, contributing to the Impressionist exhibitions, joining in the discussions at the Café Guerbois in Paris, borrowing money from an increasing circle of friends – including Manet and Zola. The substantial amounts he was now earning were spent on, amongst other things, servants for the large house at Argenteuil. Monet also made important contacts with patrons such as Hoschedé and Chocquet.

In the end circumstances and the solitary, ambitious nature of Monet's personal endeavour drew him further away from the other Impressionists. The fall of his patron Hoschedé, a decline in Monet's modest fortunes, Camille's second

MONET
Sunset at Lavacourt
oil on canvas
1880. 101.5 × 150cm
(40 × 59in)
This picture forms a sequel to the famous Impression, Sunrise.

MONET
Cliff Walk, Pourville
oil on canvas
1882. 65 × 81cm (26 × 32in)
Monet frequently went to the same
coastline of Normandy to paint,
usually alone. Monet stayed nearly
six months in the area, experimenting
with depicting the changing light
with increasing accuracy. He had
started to use boxes specially made
for him, capable of holding freshly
painted canvases.

pregnancy and, soon after, her worsening illness, led to the two families living together in a new home in Vétheuil, further along the Seine from Argenteuil. Eventually Ernest Hoschedé left the Monet-Hoschedé household, and, after the death of Camille in 1879, Monet, Jean, Camille's new baby Michel, Alice Hoschedé and her six children were left to carry on with life together as best they could.

The turmoil in his personal life, the real threat of poverty with a family of nine to support, and the withering of Monet's links to the other Impressionists, formed an inauspicious start to the 1880s. He had been too poor and depressed by the time of the fourth Impressionist exhibition in 1879 to want to exhibit, however, and the good Caillebotte, who had rented the studio where Monet had finished

the Gare St Lazare pictures, had himself collected twenty-nine works from Monet and sent them in for him. The next year Monet absented himself from the fifth Impressionist show. To the extreme disgust of Pissarro and Degas, Monet decided instead to submit to the Salon for the first time in many years.

Monet's relationship to Durand-Ruel now took on a new importance. Durand-Ruel had found him reasonably bankable in a time of economic depression and Monet was the first of the Impressionists to have a one-man show at the dealer's gallery in 1883. During the 1880s Monet at last began to make a comfortable income from his work and in 1883 he was able to move to Giverny, his last home. But his dedication to expanding his vision was untrammelled.

The search for new inspiration now took him on a series of extended travels in search of problematical landscapes. He went first to the Normandy coast, usually leaving Alice and the children behind, and then to more distant climes – the south of France, northern Italy and Norway. The intrepid artist often found himself battling with the elements. A letter to Alice from Etretat in 1885 recounts how he was working at the Manneporte, a spectacular rock formation off the northwestern coast and the subject for several paintings, when he failed to observe a huge wave which smashed him against the cliff and dragged him down in its undertow: "My first thought was that I was done for

... My boots, stockings and coat were soaked through ... the palette ... had hit me in the face and my beard was covered in blue and yellow, etc ... the worst thing was that I lost my painting which soon disintegrated along with the easel."

For an artist such as Monet who had developed an incredible sensitivity towards colour in a northern French landscape, which is subdued at the best of times and in the winter mournfully so, one might well imagine what the intense Mediterranean sun and landscape could unleash in his mind. The bright blues of the sea and sky were at first, he said, "appalling" and "beyond me": in the end of course he mastered them. During the 1880s Monet's palette was finally liberated from

any lingering attachment to natura-listic colour; the *Rocks at Belle-Île* (*Rochers à Belle-Île*), and the *Poppy Fields at Giverny* (*Champs de pivots à Giverny*) are worked and re-worked (in the studio) with thick, startlingly livid pigment. They go beyond the mere *impression* of colour values and have now become a mode of *defining* the complex emotional relationship of the artist to the scene in terms of colour.

In 1892 Ernest Hoschedé died, enabling Monet and Alice to marry. The artist had now cut down on his travels and began to devote himself once again to the landscape around his home. Continually searching for a way to paint the elusive moment, the "fugitive effect," as he put it, Monet had embarked on a multi-

MONET
Grain stacks at Sunset,
Frosty Weather
oil on canvas
1891. 65 × 100cm
(26 × 39in)
The Neo-Impressionists found Monet's works "old hat" by now, because he was merely evolving rather than radically changing direction.

MONET
Rouen Cathedral
oil on canvas 1894. 100 × 65cm
(39 × 26in) *ABOVE*

MONET
The Cathedral Fog
oil on canvas
1894. 106 × 72.5cm (42 × 29in)
*OPPOSITE Monet started his series on the
cathedral of Rouen in the late winter of
1892–93, and the following year set
himself up in the window of a shop from
where he could follow the changing light
on the medieval façade.*

canvas series of subjects, the first of
which, the *Meules* or *Grain Stacks*
(not "haystacks", they are stacks of
wheat or oats), was begun in the
mid-1880s. When the series was
due to be exhibited at Durand-
Ruel's gallery in 1891 Pissarro was
moved to complain to his son
Lucien: "All people want at the
moment is Monets, apparently he
can't paint enough to meet the
demand. The worst thing is that
they all want grain stacks at sunset!

Always the same story, everything
he does goes to America at prices of
four, five, and six thousand francs."

The series of *Meules* was thus a
stunning success, both financially
and artistically. The concept of a
group of pictures on one subject,
which had been seen as a whole,
reflected Monet's method – to
work on several canvases at once,
waiting for the light to change to
the correct quality for a particular
picture. Moreover, the series now
represented a record, in a disturbing
totality, not only of the subject
under varying conditions, but
Monet's response to it over time.
Speaking of the *Meules* series,
which he saw in 1895, the painter
Wassily Kandinsky said: "Painting
took on a fabulous strength and
splendour, and at the same time,
unconsciously, the object was
discredited as an indispensable
element of the picture." True
enough, contemporary viewers
were initially perplexed by the need
to see the whole through its parts.
The "discredited object" – in other
words making the object abstract by
repeating it in various states – is a
major consequence of Monet's
series paintings. The *Poplars* series of
1891, the *Rouen Cathedral* series
of 1894, and the *Mornings on the
Seine* of 1896–97 continue this
serial preoccupation. In the late
1890s and early 1900s Monet went
on his last travels to London (where
he had painted over 100 views of
the Thames by 1904) and his last
expedition to Venice in 1908.

As Monet's work was now
selling for substantial amounts he
could afford to realize his dream of
creating a large flower and water

garden, achieved by buying a plot adjacent to the house, diverting the stream which ran through the land and forming a water-lily pond with a Japanese bridge over it. It was in this garden that he spent the last decades of his life. Over the years the garden expanded into a wonderland of flowers of all varieties. "What I need most of all are flowers, always, always," he said. His artistic attention now turned to the waterscape offered by the lily pond. A prodigious series of *Nymphéas*, or *Water Lilies*, now followed, taking Monet into new realms of vision. As he told Geffroy in 1908: "These landscapes of water and reflections have become an obsession. It's quite beyond my

powers at this age, but I need to succeed in expressing what I feel." The consequence of this obsession was the *Nymphéas, paysages d'eau* (*Water Lilies, Waterscapes*) a series of forty-eight canvases exhibited at Durand-Ruel's in 1909. This later became a monumental concept for a huge *décoration* to be donated to the State and installed in a public building in Paris. The plan, encouraged by the politician Georges Clemenceau, was audacious and at times it seemed as though it would never happen. In 1911 Alice Monet had died and to add to his grief his son Jean died in 1914. Cared for by his step-daughter Blanche Hoschedé-Monet and with the support of

MONET
The Japanese
Bridge at Giverny
oil on canvas
1893. 97 × 117cm (38 × 46in)
ABOVE Monet had a Japanese-style bridge built over a pond he created by diverting a tributary of the local river Epte. Monet depicted this pond tirelessly until his death in 1926.

MONET
Poplars
oil on canvas
1891. 101 × 66cm (40 × 26in)
OPPOSITE The series of poplars followed immediately after the grain stacks, and was shown at Durand-Ruel's in 1892. By then, Monet's eyesight was deteriorating.

MONET
The Rose Path, Giverny
oil on canvas
1920–2. 89 × 100cm
(35 × 39in)
Monet's bad eyesight cannot entirely explain the semi-abstract style he had now reached. It often happens that ageing artists lose their stamina and produce works which do not compare favourably to their earlier ones. With Monet, this was not the case.

Clemenceau, the seventy-four-year-old artist was able to persevere with the project for the massive *décorations*.

To realize the *décorations* Monet proposed the building of a new studio specially to house the work in progress. As World War I raged around him, Monet supervised the construction of the studio and worked on the *Nymphéas* in the old studio. He had developed cataracts which made it increasingly difficult for him to discern colour, yet he carried on relentlessly. When the new studio was finished in 1916 he began what was almost a decade of unremitting work on the *décorations*. His failing eyesight meant he was frequently uncertain of what he was doing and, in despair, he destroyed several canvases. An operation in 1923 eventually restored enough of his sight for

Monet, now eighty-three and dying of cancer caused by habitual cigarette smoking, to near completion of the *décorations*. The immense work was designed to be housed in a circular or oval room and to this end the Orangerie near the Louvre was designated to house it, but not without political and personal complications on a huge scale.

Monet died on 5th December 1926, a month after his eighty-sixth birthday, with Clemenceau at his side. He had lived just long enough to see the completion of the *décorations*, his troublesome masterpiece of a gift to the French nation. As Gustave Geffroy said of the lily pond, the inspiration for his last great works:

There he found, as it were, the last word on things, if things had a first and last word. He discovered and demonstrated that everything is everywhere, and that after running round the world worshipping the light that brightens it, he knew that this light came to be reflected in all its splendour and mystery in the magical hollow surrounded by the foliage of willow and bamboo, by flowering irises and rose bushes through the mirror of water from which burst strange flowers which seem even more silent and hermetic than all the others.

Monet was famed throughout the world and his work fetched enormous prices; his persistence and stubborn devotion to his art had made his fortune. He had also outlived two wives, a son, the Second Republic, the Second Empire and all of his contemporaries including Pissarro, Degas, and Renoir.

Six months before his death he wrote: ". . . in the end the only merit I have is to have painted directly from nature before the most fugitive effects, and it still upsets me that I was responsible for the name given to a group, most of whom had nothing Impressionist about them . . ."

A series of paintings of the Japanese bridge and the garden at Giverny are among Monet's last works, apart from the *décorations*. The last canvases are covered by violent, feverish brushstrokes with an inferno of colour – the last challenges to sunlight of one of the first great Impressionists.

MONET
Nymphéas *(DETAIL)*
oil on canvas
Undated. 132 × 84cm
(52 × 33in)
Monet painted hundreds of pictures of this pond or parts of it.

renoir

GEORGE MOORE, AN ENGLISH WRITER who was reasonably close to the Impressionists during the Batignolles days, thought Pierre-Auguste Renoir possessed a certain "vulgarity", a feeling expressed, though not of course explicitly, by Renoir himself, whose eventual fame sat uneasily on the head of a self-confessed artisan. Although his ambivalent social position gave him much to be nervous about, Renoir was existentially nervy, a source of perpetual motion who would whistle incessantly whilst painting and fall into utter moroseness and depression when idle.

As an iconoclast of his own work, his dissatisfaction with the extraordinary surface effects of his "high Impressionist" period culminated in a search for classical simplicity in line and volume which lead him back to the work of Raphael, and sideways to the experiments of Cézanne. In the end he found his métier in the female figure. Even when his eyesight and rheumatic hands began to fail him, he branched out into sculpture, using an assistant, as well as tapestry design and ceramics – he had after all begun his career as a porcelain-painter.

RENOIR
Self-portrait
c.1875.
ABOVE

RENOIR
Seated Bather
oil on canvas
c.1885.
54.5 × 42cm
(22 × 17in)
OPPOSITE

LIFE AND WORKS: PIERRE-AUGUSTE RENOIR (1841–1919)

Artists do exist. But one doesn't know where to find them. An artist can do nothing if the person who asks him to produce work is blind. It is the eye of the sensualist that I wish to open.

PIERRE-AUGUSTE RENOIR

RENOIR
Bazille at Work
oil on canvas
1867. 105 × 73.5cm
(41 × 29in)
Renoir has produced an honest and forthright portrait of his close friend. The rendering is fluent, but the artist has not yet found the style to which he owes his fame.

Pierre-Auguste Renoir's father Léonard "Raynouard", as the land register of the time called him, was a tailor from Limoges who had moved to Paris in 1844 with his family. Renoir's mother, Marguerite was a dressmaker and Pierre-Auguste, born on 25th February 1841, was the sixth of seven children, two of whom died in infancy. At the age of fourteen Renoir was apprenticed in the traditional way to M. Levy, a porcelain-painter. To improve his skills he also studied drawing at a free school and when Levy's firm could no longer compete with the machine-produced porcelain-ware taking over the market and closed down in 1858, Renoir then painted fans for his brother, Henri, copying the work of Watteau, Lancret, Boucher, and Fragonard, and blinds for a M. Gilbert until he entered Charles Gleyre's atelier in 1861. A year later he met Monet, Bazille, and Sisley there. His capacity for self-improvement was formidable, and in 1862 he won a place at the Ecole des Beaux-Arts where he studied as a pupil of Gleyre's until 1864. He had also gained permission to copy in the Louvre and the Cabinet d'Estampes. In later years, when he and his friends were famous, Renoir was the only one to recognize the efforts of the good Charles Gleyre: "It was under Gleyre that I learnt my trade as a painter," he said, and in the 1880s he was to return to the techniques Gleyre had taught him. At the time, however, his relationship with Gleyre had its humorous moments. On one occasion Gleyre inspected some of Renoir's work and wryly advised him that painting shouldn't be done for one's own amusement, to which the plucky Renoir replied "If it didn't amuse me I wouldn't paint."

Renoir's career at the Ecole des Beaux-Arts was hardly spectacular; on one occasion he came fourth with an honourable mention in the perspective drawing examination, but generally his results were undistinguished. Not so his formative relationship with the other Gleyre students. In 1862 he was already accompanying them on landscape painting expeditions to the Fontainebleau Forest. "When I was young," he said nostalgically many years later, "I used to go to Fontainebleau with Sisley, with just my paint-box and the shirt on my back. We would wander round until we found a village, and sometimes come back a week later when we had run out of money." Monet, Bazille and Sisley had soon become important allies. They were all from the prosperous middle class, though Renoir, from the skilled working class, an *ouvrier de la peinture* as he called himself, had to earn a living by undertaking decorative work. As the art historian John House observes in his study of "Renoir's Worlds", when Bazille, comfortably supported by his parents, shared his studio with his friends, Monet played the role of a bohemian who had rejected parental authority, whereas Renoir simply had to seek the cheapest way he could find to live. Renoir strove to become a bourgeois through his art and his friends. His first successful submission to the Salon in 1865 was a portrait of Sisley's wealthy

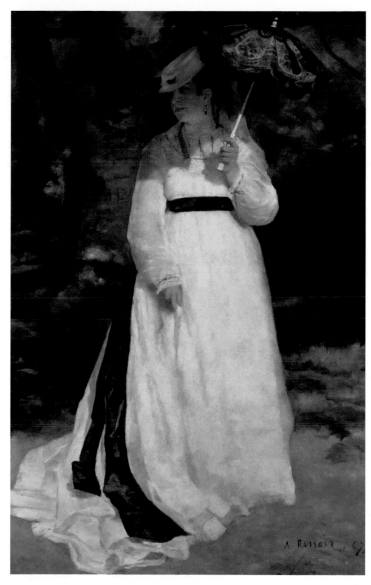

father, and the greater part of his career was to depend on patronage by and portraiture for the bourgeoisie. Yet the question of class troubled him throughout his life; his later affair with and marriage to a laundress, Aline Charigot, was kept secret from his

RENOIR
Lise
oil on canvas
1867. 181.5 × 113cm
(72 × 45in)
Painted in 1867, the portrait of the Jules Le Coeur's mistress was exhibited at the Salon the following year.

friends – Renoir was terrified that they might think of her as a lowly peasant.

By nature Renoir was a restless soul and in this respect he was later to be compared to Watteau, one of his early influences. He was also highly impressionable. Unsympathetic analyses of his work held up the considerable influence of his contemporaries, firstly Monet and later Cézanne, as proof that he was ambivalent and confused as to his own identity as an artist. To a certain extent this is true, but his talent was both convincing and original, chiefly in his portrayal of the modern life of Paris for which he is most admired.

In 1868 Renoir and Bazille moved into rooms with a studio in the Batignolles quarter of Paris. As a member of the group of future Impressionists who had gravitated towards the Batignolles and the Café Guerbois where Edouard Manet held court, Renoir was now becoming involved in the struggle for recognition. Following the

Salon's rejection of his painting *Diana the Huntress* (*Diane chasseresse*) in 1867, he had signed a petition calling for another Salon des Refusés and was soon to be a prominent member of the *Société anonyme* which launched the first Impressionist show. In 1868, he received considerable acclaim at the Salon for his painting *Lise with a Parasol* (*Lise au parasol*), which Zola thought "a successful exploration of the modern". The critic Duret had bought a previous *Lise*, also known as *The Gypsy Girl* (*La Gitane*), and Renoir's name was increasingly to be heard mentioned in connection with the avant-garde whilst his style remained subtly tailored to the Salon. Lise Tréhot, the subject of *Lise* and many more paintings to come, was the sister of Clémence Tréhot, the mistress of Jules Le Coeur, a painter and close friend of Renoir and Sisley. In 1865 Le Coeur had bought a house at Marlotte in the Fontainebleau Forest where Renoir, Sisley, and the Tréhot sisters would frequently

RENOIR

La Loge
oil on canvas
1874. 80 × 64cm
(32 × 26in)
OPPOSITE This now famous picture passed unnoticed at the first Impressionist exhibition, as did the artist's other works, although it was the first Impressionist treatment of this subject. It has since been acknowledged as a masterpiece. A work of charm and candour, the mismatching of the sitters to the setting adds to the painting's appeal. The woman was the model Nini Lopez, who does not have the allure of a high society woman. The man was Renoir's brother, Edmond, a willing accomplice in many of the artist's works.

RENOIR

La Grenouillère
oil on canvas
1869. 65 × 93cm (26 × 37in)
RIGHT Here we see people standing on the gangplank between the bank and the "camembert" from which they could watch the bathers. Renoir's brushstrokes are lighter and lack Monet's bravura handling.

RENOIR
Victor Chocquet
oil on canvas
c.1876. 46 × 36cm
(18 × 14in)
*ABOVE Chocquet, a modest civil servant
with a small private income, was a
compulsive collector of paintings.*

RENOIR
The Path in the Grass
oil on canvas
c.1875. 60 × 74cm (24 × 29in)
*RIGHT The composition of this painting
is reminiscent of the* Poppy Field
*painted by Monet two years
previously, although Monet's work
includes a greater depth of sky and
his horizon is firmly marked
by a row of trees. Here, the path
is clearly the axis of the picture,
balanced by the vertical tree off
centre. The vegetation is detailed
in Renoir's own fluttering style.*

spend the summer months. Nearby was the famous Cabaret de la mère Anthony, a country inn frequented by artists, writers, and bohemians of every hue. The Cabaret is the subject of an early picture which Renoir remembered with great pleasure. "It is not that I find the picture itself particularly exciting, but it does remind me of good old Mother Anthony and her inn at Marlotte. That was a real village inn!"

During the late 1860s Renoir's style was at a crossroads. The rapidly executed *Skaters in the Bois de Boulogne* (*Patineurs au Bois de Boulogne*) of 1868 showing the marked influence of Monet, contrasts with the sobriety of the touching double portrait of Sisley and his wife-to-be, *The Engaged Couple* (*Les Fiancés*) of the same year. In 1869 Renoir spent the summer living with his parents in Louveciennes. Nearly every day he travelled the few miles up the river to Bougival where Monet was living and together they went to paint at the popular bathing establishment known as La Grenouillère (The Froggery) on the Île-de-Croissy in the Seine. To many minds this is where Impressionism was born. The two artists worked side by side at the same views with practically the same palette and brushstrokes. A comparison of the results of that summer shows that Renoir had tried to apply a great deal of Monet's approach. The short, rapid brushstrokes and high-keyed colours employed by Monet are echoed by Renoir, but in a more uncertain fashion. Renoir's

RENOIR
Ball at the Moulin de la Galette
oil on canvas
1876. 131 × 175cm (52 × 69in)
In order to paint this composition,
Renoir called on some patient
friends. The three men on the
right are Pierre Franc-Lamy and
Norbert Goenette, both painters,
and the writer Georges Rivière.
On the bench are two sisters,
Estelle and Jeanne. The latter
was Renoir's new model, who
also posed for The Swing.
The dancer in pink is Margot
(Marguerite Legrand) with the
Cuban painter Solarès. The girls
were all from the working classes,
and the men were younger friends
of the artist.

RENOIR
The First Outing
oil on canvas
c.1876–77. 65 × 49.5cm (26 × 20in)
*ABOVE The girl is a young and
unsophisticated figure. It has been
recently discovered that Renoir had
originally painted a male figure in
profile, which occupied most of the space
now taken by the distant boxes, and
that the blue garment left of centre was
part of this man's jacket.*

RENOIR
Madame Charpentier and
Her Children
oil on canvas
1878. 154 × 190cm (61 × 75in)
*RIGHT In 1876, Renoir had the good
fortune to meet the Charpentiers, a
wealthy and influential couple.
Marguerite commissioned her own
portrait and, using her connections,
made sure that it was prominently
displayed at the Salon. However, this
did not spare the work from criticism,
some of which could be applied to much
of Renoir's work: a gifted colourist but
lacking in draughtsmanship.*

approach to the subject concen-
trates more on the crowd of figures
in the scene.

With the outbreak of the
Franco-Prussian war in July 1870,
Renoir joined the Tenth Cavalry
Regiment and was posted to
Libourne in the Bordeaux region.
There he succumbed to a severe
attack of dysentery and was rescued
by his uncle who took him to the
town of Bordeaux to recuperate. By
the end of February 1871 he was
back with his regiment and his
record states that he "conducted
himself well for the duration of the
war." By the time in April when he
had been demobilized and returned
to Paris, the Commune was in
power and the city was under siege.
Nothing could stop him painting
though, and he obtained a pass
from the Prefect of Police and
was able to leave Paris on painting
expeditions and to visit his parents
in Louveciennes.

Between 1871 and 1874
Renoir continued his close
association with Monet, visiting
him at Argenteuil during the
summers, as well as becoming more
intimately involved in the fledgling
Société anonyme; he now had a studio
in Montmartre in the rue Saint-
Georges where the *Société anonyme*
often met in 1873 to plan its first
exhibition. His style was beginning
to mature; his view of the *Pont Neuf*
of 1872, though the choice of the
subject was influenced by Monet,
presents a highly original use of
colour and contrasts strongly with a
rather dour view of a similar
subject, the *Pont des Arts*, done in
1867. Renoir's brother Edmond, a
journalist, had an interesting

anecdote about how the *Pont Neuf* was painted. The two brothers would take up residence at a little café and for ten centimes each they could sit with two coffees for hours. Whilst Auguste painted, Edmond scribbled, occasionally venturing on to the bridge to engage passers-by in conversation so that Auguste could sketch them in situ. In another vein, the *Morning Ride in the Bois de Boulogne* (*L'Allée cavalière au Bois de Boulogne*) of 1873, an enormous canvas eight and a half by seven and a half feet, is an attempt by Renoir to paint a large-scale

RENOIR
The Umbrellas
oil on canvas
c.1885. 180.5 × 115cm (71 × 45in)
OPPOSITE Many artists begin with a tighter style which becomes somewhat looser as they gain experience and self-confidence. The opposite was true in Renoir's case: he felt he had reached a dead-end, and his observation of the neat contours and finish of painters such as Raphael prompted him to work with more discipline and care.

RENOIR
Luncheon of the Boating Party
oil on canvas
1880–81. 130 × 173cm
(51 × 68in)

ABOVE On the left, holding a small dog, is Aline Charigot, Renoir's future companion and wife. Alphonse Fournaise, the son of the establishment's owner, stands next to her. The girl leaning on the balustrade is a model. The man wearing a top hat is Charles Ephrussi, a wealthy writer and collector. Angèle, another model, is seated, drinking. The painter Lhote leans forward to talk to the actress Jeanne Samary, and the painter Caillebotte, another close friend of Renoir's, wearing a singlet and a straw hat, is seated in the foreground. This was the last of Renoir's crowd scenes, and one of his most popular works ever.

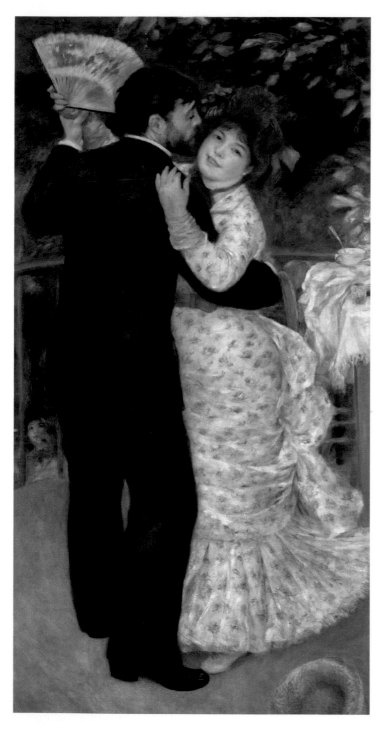

work with the Salon in mind. Despite this ambition, it was rejected and appeared at the Salon des Refusés.

When the accounts for the first exhibition of the *Société anonyme* were drawn up after the disastrous exhibition of 1874 each member of the society owed 184 francs 50 centimes; few paintings had been sold, although Renoir had managed to avoid most of the hysterical criticism aimed at colleagues such as Monet, Pissarro, and Degas. One of the pictures Renoir exhibited, *La Loge*, the first of several paintings on this theme and now considered an icon of Impressionism, was later bought by Père Martin, a rather dubious small-time dealer, for the sum of 425 francs. This was not an insubstantial amount for an impecunious artist – in any case Renoir owed it in back rent – but a Salon picture by Meissonier, for example, could fetch 40,000 francs. In December the *Société* terminated, with Renoir as the chairman. The next year, resourceful as ever, he had the idea of a joint auction with Monet, Sisley, and Morisot to be held at the Hôtel Drouot. The newly named Impressionists were by now so infamous that there were demonstrations when the paintings went on show in March. Renoir sold twenty works for an average of 112 francs, with some going for as little as 50 francs. Thankfully Renoir's precarious position was now helped by the fortunate arrival on the scene of the collector Victor Chocquet who commissioned several portraits of his family which kept the artist financially afloat.

RENOIR
Dance in the Country
oil on canvas
1882–83. 180 × 90cm
(71 × 35in)
*OPPOSITE Renoir painted three nearly
life-size dancing couples between 1882
and 1883. The differences are quite
marked between the relaxed and happy
Aline in* Dance in the Country, *who
was putting on weight, and the more
composed, elegant couple of* Dance in
the City, *for which the young model
Maria Clémentine (later known as the
painter Suzanne Valadon) was the
model. Renoir's old friend Lhote, who
had posed for several other pictures, is
the partner in both panels.*

RENOIR
Landscape at Guernsey
oil on canvas
1883. 46 × 56cm (18 × 22in)
*ABOVE Renoir and his family spent
a month on the Channel Island
of Guernsey in the late summer of
1883, where he painted around
fifteen pictures, many of them
intended as sketches to be used
for studio compositions later on.*

RENOIR
Aline Charigot
oil on canvas
c.1885. 65 × 54cm (26 × 21in)
ABOVE The rendering of this portrait, which Renoir kept all his life, evokes the diagonals of Cézanne.

RENOIR
The Apple Seller
oil on canvas
c.1890. 66 × 54cm
(26 × 21in)
OPPOSITE In this rustic scene, Aline poses with a young girl and probably her son, Pierre, seated to the right. This is the most elaborate of three pictures Renoir painted on the same theme.

In 1875 Renoir had rented for a hundred francs a month the dilapidated outbuildings of an old folly with a garden in the rue Cortot as a studio. The next summer his friends Pierre Lamey, Frédéric Cordey, and Georges Rivière often joined him in outings to a popular haunt, the Moulin de la Galette – a dance hall and café beneath one of the last remaining windmills of Montmartre. According to Georges Rivière, in the mornings he and the others would help Renoir carry his canvas and easel round the corner to the dance hall where the artist spent the summer painting a large scene of the crowds there now known as the *Ball at the Moulin de la Galette* – one of several masterpieces he was to produce that summer. Although he certainly worked on it *in situ*, posing his friends and acquaintances, including Rivière, it was prepared with sketches and finished in the studio in the rue Cortot. Nevertheless, it is Renoir's first large-scale figure painting to deploy the swift technique he had been perfecting since the summer of 1869 at La Grenouillère with Monet. The dappled sunlight is a particular feature of this period, as is the abandoned use of colour in the shadows. The painting was shown at the third Impressionist group exhibition the next year when a critic under the pseudonymous name of Flor O'Squarr said of Renoir's painting:

The painter had caught perfectly the raucous and slightly bohemian atmosphere of this open-air dance hall, perhaps the last of its kind in Paris . . . The harsh sunlight is

filtered through the greenery, sets the blonde hair and pink cheeks of the girls aglow and makes their ribbons sparkle. The joyful light fills every corner of the canvas and even the shadows reflect it. The whole painting shimmers like a rainbow and makes one think of the dainty Chinese princess described by Heinrich Heine: her greatest pleasure in life was to tear up satin and silk with her polished jade-like nails and watch the shreds of yellow, blue, and pink drift away in the breeze like so many butterflies.

This summer also produced the equally famous *The Swing* (*La Balançoire*), thought to have been painted in the garden at the rue Cortot. A young woman from the neighbourhood, Jeanne, posed on the swing (and is also present in *The Ball*). The same dappled light is more intensely expressed here and imbues the picture with that insouciant charm of which only Renoir (who had of course once copied Watteau for a living) was capable. Zola was so taken with the painting that he used it in his novel *Une Page d'amour* of 1878, where the heroine is "standing on the very edge of the swing and holding the ropes, with her arms outstretched . . . she was wearing a grey dress decorated with mauve bows . . . That day the sunlight was like light-coloured dust in the pale sky . . . "

Towards the end of the 1870s Renoir began to become less involved with the Impressionists as a group. After the third Impressionist exhibition in 1877 he forsook the group and began to concentrate on the Salon as an outlet for his work. His new

RENOIR
Landscape
oil on canvas
c.1895. 46 × 33cm
(18 × 13in)
ABOVE Renoir was deliberately trying to adapt Cézanne's diagonal brushstrokes to his own style and to adapt his colour harmony. This is an atypical work, more vigorous than his usual pictures.

RENOIR
Girls at the Piano
oil on canvas
1892. 116 × 90cm
(46 × 35in)
OPPOSITE Renoir, at last an established artist, was asked by the French government to provide a substantial painting for the national collection, for which he was to be paid 4,000 francs.

patrons the Charpentiers were now beginning to commission portraits as well as decorations for their town house in Paris, and Renoir scored a relative success at the Salon of 1879 with the *Portrait of Madame Charpentier and her Children*. Marcel Proust includes a long description of the painting in *Le Temps retrouvé* (*Time Regained*) and likens it to "Titian at his best". The most favourable reviews concentrated on Renoir's use of colour, which was by now quite brilliant. The steady development of what became known as his rainbow palette can be seen in perhaps its most scintillating and impressionistic form in *Boating on the Seine* (*Canotage sur la Seine*), (also known as *The Skiff*, or *The Seine at Asnières*, though it was probably painted at Chatou), produced around the same time as the Charpentier portrait. The painting shows an almost text-book application of Chevreul's principles of simultaneous colour contrast. Renoir uses only seven pigments and white, applying them to the canvas in bold, practically unmixed patches to convey an impression of sheer luminosity.

It is ironic and typical of Renoir's nature that at a time he was producing veritable icons of Impressionist art he was also beginning to have serious doubts about his own ability. The financial need to paint an increasing number of society portraits no doubt aggravated the strain on his own artistic judgment of himself. To make matters worse, in 1880 he and Monet had fallen out with Degas, who they suspected was highjack-ing the Impressionist exhibitions

and populating them with his protégés. A trip to Algiers, his first abroad, in the spring of 1881 reassured him of the direction he was taking as an Impressionist and he was soon back in France at Chatou and Bougival painting masterpieces such as *Luncheon of the Boating Party* (*Le Déjeuner des canoteurs*) with rekindled vigour. But by October he had left for Italy, writing to Mme Charpentier: "I have suddenly become a traveller and I am in a fever to see the Raphaels . . . "

Renoir had gone to Algeria in the Romantic footsteps of Delacroix, but he now approached Italy seeking the formal classicism of Raphael, which he was to find in the great decorations at the Villa Farnesina. He was also profoundly influenced by what he called "the grandeur and simplicity" of the ancient Pompeian wall paintings in Naples. It was some time, however, before these new influences could reconcile themselves in his work: "... it's all a mess. I'm still making a mess and I'm forty years old," he wrote to Durand-Ruel from Italy in November 1881.

Renoir returned to France in January 1882 and joined Cézanne at l'Estaque in the south of France where the two went on landscape expeditions and Renoir caught pneumonia. He had also caught something of Cézanne's vision of the hidden structure of planes and lines in nature. The confluence and confusion of the diverse influences at work on Renoir can be seen in *The Umbrellas* (*Les Parapluies*), which shows him struggling to reconcile a linear style with Impressionist

RENOIR
The Artist's House at Essoyes
oil on canvas
1906. 31 × 40cm (12 × 16in)
*ABOVE Renoir's late style became
increasingly loose, which is partly
explained by his failing eyesight and
the crippling arthritis which in the end
confined him to a wheelchair.*

RENOIR
Bather (Eurydice)
oil on canvas
1895–1900. 116 × 89cm
(46 × 35in)
*OPPOSITE This nude is not any nude, it
is a goddess in the nude. Here, four tiny
figures in the background provide a
pretext for the title. Renoir had by then
completely returned to his "soft" style,
which he attempted to control only when
he was painting commissioned portraits.*

brushwork. More importantly, in the mid-1880s there is a new concentration on the female nude as a vehicle for expressing light, colour and form. He told Berthe Morisot that, "the nude seemed to be one of the most essential forms of art." Renoir's fellow Impressionists and the dealer Durand-Ruel were mystified by the new linear style and said so, but Renoir persisted in his experiments with a series of *Bathers*, culminating in the monumental *Bathers* (*Baigneuses*) of 1887. His interest in the female form had also taken a new turn in 1885 when his mistress, Aline Charigot, bore his first son Pierre, prompting the artist to produce the Raphael-inspired

Maternity, developing the simplified theme of the *Bathers*.

Renoir's "*manière aigre*" ("sour period") as he called it, came to an end in the late 1880s. After a trip to Spain in 1892 he drew new inspiration from Velazquez. The work of the eighteenth-century French painters Watteau and Fragonard which he had copied on to fans in his youth also came to influence him and he rediscovered the delicate virtues of Corot whose work was now much in demand by collectors. The insistence on line gradually softened but his humanistic concern with the figure remained overwhelmingly important.

In 1902 Renoir and Aline moved to the south of France

where the warm climate eased the severe arthritis which was making it difficult for him to paint. He could now "only paint broadly" as he put it, and the nerve in his right eye was partially atrophied. Undaunted by his illness he embarked on a series of sculptures echoing the nude figure paintings, though he had to use the hands of an assistant to model them.

Aline died in 1915 of a heart attack caused by overweight; she was a compulsive eater. Renoir died on 3rd December 1919 and was buried next to her in Essoyes.

In 1900 he had been made a Knight of the Légion d'Honneur, and in the last year of his life he became a Commander of the Légion d'Honneur, a triumphant honour for a humble "*ouvrier de la peinture*".

RENOIR
The Bathers
oil on canvas
c.1918–19. 110 × 160cm
(43 × 63in)

With this work, the ailing painter was determined to make a final statement, showing nude women in a landscape, two of his favourite subjects. Crippled by illness, he had the easel set up in such a manner that he could reach any part of this large canvas. Pain sometimes interrupted his work. His son Jean stated that his father "considered it as a final achievement. He thought he had summed up in it the research of his whole life", though to many people the painting is more often seen as the final work of a weakening artist. Georges Duthuit probably echoed the modern public's feeling when he wrote that "Renoir's late work was short of imagination, and deprived of any dramatic sense . . . so that one finds something slack and overblown".

Sisley.

F ROM COMFORTABLE BEGINNINGS as the son of a successful English businessman in Paris, Alfred Sisley's story is one of tragic decline and late success. After the crash of his father's firm in the Franco-Prussian War, Sisley and his family were reduced to a state of penury which persisted almost to the end of his life when cancer of the throat killed him at the age of sixty.

Part of Sisley's lack of wordly success is undoubtedly due to the subdued and comparatively unspectacular nature of the landscapes which were his almost exclusive preoccupation. Had he been interested in the colourful effects of dazzling sunlight or violent seascapes he may have enjoyed more attention than the belated admiration of a small number of collectors and connoisseurs. Yet his work is dramatic and powerful in its own way and his snowscapes, especially, convey something of the unremitting sadness which plagued him.

RENOIR
Alfred Sisley
1874.
ABOVE

SISLEY
The Road from
Mantes to
Choisy-le-Roi
oil on canvas
1872. 46 × 55cm
(18 × 22in)
OPPOSITE

LIFE AND WORKS: ALFRED SISLEY (1839–1899)

The light of glory will never shine on his work in his lifetime.

GUSTAVE GEFFROY ON SISLEY, 1894

SISLEY
St Martin Canal, Paris
oil on canvas
1870. 50 × 65cm
(20 × 26in)
Sisley, like most of his Impressionist friends, was interested in depicting water and sky, the two elements which best suited their stylistic research, and amongst the most difficult to render.

Alfred Sisley was born in Paris on 30th October 1839 to affluent English parents. His father, William, ran a business exporting artificial flowers to South America and his mother, Felicia, was well known as a society lady interested in the arts and music. At the age of eighteen Alfred was sent to London to prepare for a career in business, but his four years there were not solely devoted to the commodities market; he spent a great deal of his time in the art galleries and museums dreaming of being an artist. The works of Constable and Turner attracted him especially, and it was in landscape that he was to make his name.

In 1862 Sisley returned to Paris from a trip and persuaded his parents to consent to his pursuing a career as an artist and in October he joined Gleyre's atelier. By December he was enjoying a dinner party given by Bazille at which the other guests included Monet and Renoir. By the next Easter the budding Impressionists had all left Gleyre's, and Sisley and his friends were to be found on the edge of the Fontainebleau Forest at Chailly painting landscapes *en plein air*. And this is what Sisley was to concentrate on for the rest of his life, combining the English tradition of landscape painting with the new techniques evolving amongst the young Impressionists.

By 1866 Sisley was exhibiting two works at his first Salon. He had been working in close contact with Monet, but unlike Renoir, who was to incorporate much of Monet's technique into his early work, Sisley had already developed a more subdued palette, which in many ways suited his calm and reserved temperament. Shortly after the 1866 Salon he married a young Parisienne, Marie Lescouezec, who was to bear him two children, Pierre and Jeanne. Two years later, when the Sisleys were living in the rue de la Paix in the Batignolles, Renoir painted a large-scale double portrait of them which conveys something of the gentleness of Sisley and his devotion to his wife. In the late 1860s Sisley was increasingly part of the Batignolles

Group meeting in the Café Guerbois, and like Bazille he was essentially a man of leisure, painting when and as he liked and under no pressure to achieve financial success with his work. Nevertheless he was to be a founding member of the *Société anonyme* in 1873, by which time his life had taken a drastically different course.

The Franco-Prussian War of 1870–71 proved to be the downfall of William Sisley and inaugurated a long period of struggle for his son, Alfred, and his young family. Sisley's father had been taken ill and his business had crumbled; when he died in 1871 the family was ruined and Sisley was now forced to paint for a living. Fortunately Monet and Pissarro, who had met the sympathetic dealer Durand-Ruel in London during the war, introduced him to Sisley in 1872 and he was assured of a moderate number of sales, but not enough to regain his previous leisured lifestyle. Sisley's post-war output increased exponentially as he painted the landscapes around his home in Louveciennes.

When the first Impressionist exhibition opened in 1874 Sisley was represented by five paintings.

SISLEY
The Bridge at Argenteuil
oil on canvas
1872. 39 × 60cm
(15 × 24in)
Argenteuil is closely associated with Monet, who lived there and made well over 175 pictures of the area.

SISLEY
Regattas at Molesey
oil on canvas
1874. 66 × 91.5cm (26 × 36in)
*ABOVE During a trip to England,
Sisley painted pictures similar to
Monet's work at Argenteuil.*

SISLEY
The Road at Louveciennes, Winter
oil on canvas
1874. 38 × 46.5cm (15 × 18in)
*OPPOSITE As with Pissarro and Monet,
Sisley liked to paint snowy
landscapes, and indeed his style
at the time was close to that of
Pissarro and Guillaumin, plain
and simple compared with most
of Monet's works.*

Perhaps fittingly, for Sisley did not court scandal, they were overshadowed by the "tongue-lickings" of Monet and the other "scandalous" paintings. Monet's influence was in fact discernible in Sisley's work; he was beginning to use brighter pigment in the broken patches which characterized the work of Monet, Renoir, and Pissarro during the 1870s and early 1880s. A trip to England in July 1874 produced some of Sisley's most colourful views of the Thames and the regattas at Hampton Court.

Sisley continued to exhibit with the Impressionists in 1876, 1877, and 1882. Between 1874 and 1877 he lived with his family at Marly-le-Roi, and it was here that he produced a series of his finest paintings of the floods which periodically inundated the area. The critic Georges Rivière, writing in the influential, short-lived, Impressionist organ *l'Impressionniste*, said of Sisley: "In all his [canvases] one discovers the same taste, the

SISLEY
Spring at Veneux
oil on canvas
1880. 73 × 90cm
(29 × 35in)
RIGHT Sisley's pictures were not as strongly individual as those of the other Impressionist painters.

SISLEY
The Road to Versailles
oil on canvas
1875. 47 × 38cm
(19 × 15in)
BELOW This road, linking Marly to Versailles since the seventeeth century, was a favourite theme for Pissarro, Renoir and Sisley.

same finesse, the same tranquillity . . . " The effects of light reflected by water under a dull grey sky and the melancholy aspects of the snowscape characterize Sisley's own depressed state of mind at this time. He was in permanent financial crisis, alleviated only by Durand-Ruel and the patrons that the prospering Renoir had cultivated, the wealthy Charpentiers, and the *pâtissier* Eugène Murer, who invited Sisley and his wife to his restaurant every Wednesday along with Guillaumin, Renoir and the famous colour merchant Père Tanguy.

By the end of the 1870s Sisley was still as desperate as ever for money. Several arrangements whereby he would be paid in advance for a number of canvases helped him eke out a living, but in 1879 he decided to renounce the Impressionist exhibitions and try his luck with the Salon once again. "I am tired," he wrote to Théodore Duret, "of vegetating as I have been doing for so long. The moment has come to make a decision. It is true

SISLEY
Flood at Port Marly
oil on canvas
1876. 60 × 81cm (24 × 32in)
One in a series, this is not an alarming scene of distressed people trapped in their homes, but a peaceful and bucolic one where the water is seen as a soothing element in which the houses are reflected.

that our exhibitions have served to make us known, and as such they have been very useful, but I think we ought not isolate ourselves much longer. The time is still far off when we can do without the prestige which the Salon offers. Thus I have resolved to submit to the Salon. If I am accepted, and there is still a chance this year, I think I will be able to get things sorted out . . . "

But Sisley was rejected by the Salon and then evicted from the house in Sèvres where the family had been living since 1877. With the help of Charpentier other lodgings were found and throughout the 1880s, when the Sisley's lived in the Fontainebleau area, the artist's fortunes slowly began to revive. Never very keen on self-promotion, Sisley had worked quietly in the country. His landscapes were, however, greatly admired by his friends and critics, as well as several dealers; and by the early 1890s he was able to find a growing, if modest market for his work. This now featured series of

SISLEY
Farmyard at St Mammet
oil on canvas
1885. 73 × 93cm (29 × 37in)
*ABOVE Sisley's style here is more
compact than in his other landscapes
of this period, but he still uses short
strokes to suggest the texture of the
ground and of the tiled roof.*

SISLEY
Landscape with a River
oil on canvas
1881. 54 × 73cm
(21 × 29in)
*RIGHT The light, lively brushstrokes in
this landscape were not typical of Sisley's
style, and show his attempt at diversity.*

SISLEY
The Loing Canal
oil on canvas
1892. 73 × 93cm
(29 × 37in)
ABOVE Sisley painted at least ten views of the canal, which was not far from his home at Moret.

SISLEY
The Church at Moret
oil on canvas
1894. 100 × 82cm
(39 × 32in)
RIGHT In this picture, one of a series echoing the famous Rouen cathedrals painted by Monet the same year, Sisley has also chosen the medieval façade of his local church to render the effect of light and shade.

paintings of the same subject, particularly the church at Moret where the family finally settled. In the mid-1890s, when Monet and Renoir were selling at huge prices, Pissarro in fact complained to his son Lucien: "Doesn't Monet sell at a high price, and Renoir and Degas too? But Sisley and I are still bringing up the rear of the Impressionists."

In 1897, despite severe rheumatism brought on by long hours painting snowscapes *en plein air* – some of his most beautiful works – Sisley set out on a tour of southern England and Wales, producing several landscapes; but on his return to Moret another, fatal illness began to take hold of him. He was dying of throat cancer. On 31st December 1898 he wrote to his doctor: "I have given up, my dear friend, I have lost all my energy; I can barely get into my armchair so they can make the bed. I can't move my head anymore because of the swelling in my neck, my throat, and around my eyes. I don't think this can go on much longer. However, if you know of someone you can trust and who won't charge me more than 100 or 200 francs, I will see him . . ." A brief remission followed in the new year. However, a week before his death Sisley summoned Claude Monet to take his leave and to entrust his affairs to him. The artist whom Pissarro had called "a great and beautiful painter" died on 29th January 1899 and was buried on a cold grey day in the cemetery at Moret-sur-Loing; the ceremony was attended by a few friends including Monet and Renoir.

INDEX

Heitor Villa-Lobos

ARIA
from: Bachianas Brasilieras, No. 5

JAMES GALWAY

Piano part by Phillip Moll
Transcribed for Flute and Piano

GREAT PERFORMER'S EDITION

AMP 7787

ISBN 978-0-634-01388-1

Associated Music Publishers, Inc.

DISTRIBUTED BY

HAL•LEONARD®
CORPORATION
7777 W. BLUEMOUND RD. P.O. BOX 13819 MILWAUKEE, WI 53213

Aria
from: Bachianas Brasilieras No. 5

Piano part by
Phillip Moll

Heitor Villa-Lobos
Transcribed by James Galway

AMP-7787

Flute

Aria
from: Bachianas Brasilieras No. 5

Heitor Villa-Lobos
Transcribed by James Galway

AMP-7787